D1502610

THE
UNWRITTEN
RULES

THE UNWRITTEN RULES

The Six Skills You Need to Get Promoted to the Executive Level

John Beeson

JOSSEY-BASS
A Wiley Imprint
www.josseybass.com

Published by Jossey-Bass
A Wiley Imprint
989 Market Street, San Francisco, CA 94103-1741—www.josseybass.com

Jossey-Bass books and products are available through most bookstores. To contact Jossey-Bass directly call our Customer Care Department within the U.S. at 800-956-7739, outside the U.S. at 317-572-3986, or fax 317-572-4002.

Jossey-Bass also publishes its books in a variety of electronic formats. Some content that appears in print may not be available in electronic books.

Library of Congress Cataloging-in-Publication Data

Beeson, John.
  The unwritten rules : the six skills you need to get promoted to the executive level / John Beeson.
      p. cm.
  Includes bibliographical references and index.
  ISBN 978-0-470-58578-8 (hardback); ISBN 978-0-470-88997-8 (ebk);
ISBN 978-0-470-88998-5 (ebk); ISBN 978-0-470-88999-2 (ebk)
  1. Promotions. 2. Executives-Promotions. 3. Career development. I. Title.
  HF5549.5.P7B44 2010
  658.4'09—dc22

                                                          2010024716

Printed in the United States of America
FIRST EDITION
HB Printing   10 9 8 7 6 5 4 3 2 1

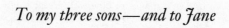

To my three sons—and to Jane

CONTENTS

Contents

CHAPTER 1

Deciphering the Code

t happens almost every day in large organizations: an
executive promotion is announced. And someone else
from your company—not you—gets the job or a new
executive is hired from the outside. The organization looks
for winners and losers, and the rumor mill goes into high
gear. Was the choice based on politics, or has the old-boy
network reared its ugly head again? Your boss and human
resource staff attempt to massage your ego. It's a matter
of experience, they say, or "fit." "They were looking for
someone with a little more" something. "Hang in there,"
they tell you. "Your time will come."

Perhaps you've experienced this situation personally. Unfortunately, in today's organizations, your career
aspirations will often collide with the reality that companies offer few guideposts for advancing to the executive
level. As predictable career paths have become more or
less extinct in most organizations, managers committed to

career growth are often left to their own devices to determine how to advance their careers. Even in companies that devote considerable time to succession planning and talent development, the messages to aspiring executives are often vague and contradictory. Your boss may find it hard to articulate exactly what it is that is holding you—an otherwise top-performing manager—back from promotion. Or the issues affecting your ability to move up the ladder have been discussed and identified by your superiors, but they hesitate to provide direct feedback for fear of demotivating a valued manager the company doesn't want to lose.

Even more frustrating, perhaps, are those instances when—having been passed over for an opportunity—your boss or an HR staff member does provide feedback, but the messages are overly diplomatic and not especially valuable to you. Broad comments about "leadership" or "communication skills" can mask specific underlying concerns on their part. Certainly it is human nature not to want to hurt someone's feelings—and those who make executive placement decisions are justifiably concerned about wanting to retain solid performers. But avoiding direct and candid feedback leaves those who aspire to executive levels at a severe disadvantage in terms of managing their careers and accomplishing their career goals.

Politics, personal relationships, and even cronyism on occasion do play a role in executive placements. However, more often these decisions are made based on the decision makers' sense, albeit intuitive, of whether a manager can succeed at higher levels within the organization. According to Susan Peters, vice president of executive development and chief learning officer at General Electric, a company widely recognized for its ability to develop strong leaders, "The reasons behind an executive's success or failure rarely relate to technical skills or specific experience. Rather, it's almost always the leadership, the soft skills."

This book seeks to decode these leadership criteria—the unwritten rules—that companies use to make decisions about who gets promoted versus those whose careers become stalled—or worse.[1] Although perhaps "soft" as opposed to "hard" areas of knowledge and experience, these unwritten rules are not purely stylistic. Rather, they are critical skills that relate to the fundamental tasks of senior leadership.

At the end of the day, promotional decisions are based on the level of confidence that you have been able to breed in your bosses—those who make the ultimate call. Although to some extent subjective, the critical factors that underlie such confidence can be identified. Outstanding job performance is important, of course, but success at one level of the organization is an imperfect predictor of the ability to succeed at higher levels of responsibility. Decision makers look for more.

Mike Peterson's story is a classic example of how outstanding performance was not enough to ensure career advancement.[2] Mike was frustrated and extremely upset: his boss had just informed him that the company had decided to hire an executive from a competitor to take over as general manager of Global Technologies Company's Systems Group, exactly the kind of position Mike had set his sights on. In fact, this was the second time in three years that he had not been considered for a general manager position. Mike had joined Global Technologies eighteen years ago right out of college and had hoped to spend his entire career with the company. However, after this second missed opportunity, he was rapidly coming to the conclusion that he needed to contact the headhunters who had called over the years and alert them to his desire to look outside. Sadly, that seemed to be the only way he could achieve the career goals he had set for himself.

Mike thought of his years of hard work and the consistent record of results he had produced for the company. He was confident of his leadership skills and the level of his team's morale. Whenever the company conducted employee opinion surveys, his group always scored near the top, and he made a point of surveying his troops about his leadership style every two years. He prided himself on having volunteered to serve as the test site for virtually every major corporate initiative over the past five years, and each program had been implemented flawlessly.

Given the top performance reviews he received every year, Mike couldn't understand why he hadn't at least been a candidate for these two promotions. He had tried on several occasions to get feedback on what was holding him back from cracking the GM level. Each time his boss and his boss's manager had assured him of his bright future with the company and that "his time would come" if he just continued to perform the way he always had. When he pressed for ways he could improve his chances of moving ahead, the response was always phrased in general terms: he needed to increase his communication skills and "executive presence" as well as exert leadership more broadly across the company. The feedback didn't make sense to Mike since his survey results always indicated that he was an effective communicator and strong leader of his people. He was even prepared to take a lateral move to a position at the same level within the company if that would increase his exposure to more senior executives and help him get where he wanted. However, at this point, he felt stumped and stymied. It looked as if it was time to find greener pastures outside Global Technologies.

In fact Mike had been seriously considered for the last two GM openings. Although he was in many respects highly qualified, there were genuine reasons he did not get the nod. Behind the feedback he had received regarding "exerting broader leadership" were concerns about his ability to work with peers in other parts of the company. Although routinely described by those in other groups as a "nice guy," he could be overly competitive. As a result, conflict with corporate groups tended to last too long and get in the way of major cross-functional efforts. In addition, although people enjoyed working on Mike's team, there were concerns that he hired good but not great staff members and that he tended to cover for mediocre performance on the part of some direct reports. Over time he had earned the loyalty of his people in part because working for him was comfortable. However, he didn't challenge members of his team to become top performers. These were issues that had never fully surfaced in the leadership surveys he had conducted over the years since he surveyed members of his group—who liked his somewhat undemanding style—and neglected to get input from peers and senior managers across the company.

Behind the feedback about executive presence lay question marks regarding Mike's strategic abilities. Unquestionably Mike was considered rock solid in his ability to implement major new initiatives within his organization. However, the CEO and head of human resources had not seen Mike's ability to generate breakthrough strategies that could help the company leapfrog its competition. Mike was a master of continuous improvement. Nothing was ever good enough, and he enlisted his team in constantly ratcheting up performance in every existing business activity. However, the CEO had never seen Mike come up with big, new ideas and drive the kind of large-scale change that would produce a significant jump in performance.

There was no doubt that he was a valuable player who could have a long career in a number of roles at Global Technologies. The CEO had spoken to Mike's bosses over the years about Mike's abilities, and although there was tacit consensus regarding his shortcomings, they were concerned about providing feedback that was too specific for fear of demotivating a key contributor. Besides, what were the chances that Mike could develop strategic gears at this point in his career? Mike had enjoyed a positive working relationship with his current boss for several years, and they made a great team. His boss was acknowledged throughout the company as a visionary leader who could create effective strategies, and Mike was seen as the classic number 2 person who made sure that each new strategy was fully implemented. Their unit was producing terrific results, so why break up a winning pair?

According to the CEO, Mike exemplified the broader executive development challenge confronting Global Technologies. Based on the head of HR's analysis and given expected retirements, the company faced attrition at the senior executive level of at least 50 percent over the next five years. There was no doubt that Mike was an important manager to hold onto. However, he and too many of his peers lacked the vision and boldness to succeed as senior executives—especially given the growing complexity of the company's business and new entrants into the industry. The only solution seemed to be gearing up the company's external recruiting effort.

THE UNWRITTEN RULES: AN OVERVIEW

Mike Peterson was a victim of insufficient feedback from his superiors. He was not aware—or hadn't been made aware—of the unwritten rules, the too-often-unspecified criteria that companies use to determine who gets promoted to the executive level. As Mike's story suggests, while in certain situations promotions to the executive level are made for specific business reasons (for example, maintaining continuity with key customers or promoting someone with experience in integrating a new acquisition), more often such decisions are based on a set of abilities that collectively breed confidence on the part of decision makers concerning an individual's ability to succeed at the executive level.

Companies such as Global Technologies often create leadership models that list important leadership requirements—such as customer focus, teamwork, and collaboration—they are looking for in their executives. Such models are typically reviewed in a company's management training programs and are often reflected in 360-degree feedback surveys such as the one that Mike Peterson conducted. Although these models are useful for general performance feedback, they rarely zero in on the critical selection factors used for C-suite-level placements. They include a number of "nice to haves": leadership skills that are certainly valuable but not those most critical to success at the executive level. Equally important, they neglect to distinguish between the aspects of leadership that are fundamental at the executive level and those that are important at lower levels within the organization. For example, Mike's ability to create team morale and a sense of cohesion within his team is highly valued by most companies at the middle management level. However, at the executive level, the ability to spot and attract talent is viewed as the key to building management strength, and this is a skill that Mike has yet to demonstrate.

Mike's story—the lack of sufficient feedback about where he stood in terms of his company's unwritten rules of advancement—is all too common in most organizations. Most senior executives are aware of the frustration that people like Mike feel, but they figure that the Mikes of the organization will "get over it." While executives such as Global Technologies' CEO bemoan their company's lack of leadership strength, too many miss the fact that this lack of specific feedback has a significant negative impact on the company's ability to develop leadership talent for the future. Although they don't show up on a company's income statement, the costs to organizations of not making explicit these unwritten rules of executive advancement are real nonetheless. They include

- The hard dollars spent on recruiting unnecessarily from outside the organization. According to a number of studies, the failure rate of new employees at the middle management level and above approaches 50 percent at many companies.[3]

- The soft-dollar costs of slowing the career growth of upwardly aspiring managers at the same time that organizations in a broad range of sectors (business, health care, and nonprofits) express concern about an impending leadership gap created by the number of baby boom–era executives in the process of retiring compared to the size of the age group poised to succeed them.[4]

- The unwanted loss of potential leaders to other companies due to ambiguous signals regarding their career prospects. Such departures not only result in an immediate loss of productivity within the company but also trigger a vicious cycle of expensive and relatively high-risk external recruitment.

Over the past thirty years, I've observed hundreds of executive placement decisions in a wide variety of organizations. I've served as a consultant to some of the largest and best-regarded companies in the world and have been responsible for succession planning and executive development at two major companies. As a consultant, I've advised CEOs and boards of directors on succession planning and executive selection, assessed and coached scores of senior executives and high-potential managers, and participated in numerous executive promotion and placement decisions. In addition, in preparation for writing this book, I conducted candid, off-the-record interviews with the heads of human resource and succession planning at twenty large corporations with excellent reputations for the strength of their leadership talent. In the interviews, I asked each person to zero in on the factors that are central to decisions in their company about who gets promoted to the C-suite level.

Along the way I've witnessed the good, the bad, and the ugly: talented executives who emerge from the pack and take on significant executive responsibilities; "can't miss" future executives whose careers have stalled unexpectedly and in some cases flamed out; and ambitious managers who, when their careers hit the wall, became frustrated, marginalized in terms of impact, and consigned to backwater assignments.

In the process I've observed that in the great majority of companies, the factors used in deciding on promotions to the executive level fall into three categories:

1. *Nonnegotiable factors*—those capabilities you must display to even be considered as a candidate

2. *Deselection factors*—characteristics that prevent you from being a serious candidate

3. *Core selection factors*—those capabilities that, after all the discussion is over, are most critical in decisions about who advances to the executive level

Taken together, these factors comprise the unwritten rules that govern executive advancement in most companies.

Clearly, certain factors are nonnegotiable. You won't be considered if you haven't developed a strong, consistent track record of performance or if there is a concern about your ethics, integrity, or character. Also nonnegotiable are a strong work ethic and the drive to assume higher levels of responsibility—as well as a willingness to deal with pressure and be held accountable for results, both good and bad. A final nonnegotiable is the drive to lead. Many managers say they aspire to senior-level positions because of the rewards and prestige that come with them. However, only a relative few truly desire to be ultimately responsible for the kinds of decisions that determine business success and affect the livelihood of people within the organization. And this willingness to make difficult, often unpopular decisions and be held accountable for the outcome is the true test of leadership.

Beyond these nonnegotiables, certain deselection factors will prevent you from even being considered for an executive-level position in most organizations. Although having excellent interpersonal skills won't guarantee success at the executive level, truly weak interpersonal skills or treating others insensitively or with abrasiveness will impede the ability to lead others. We've all seen our share of difficult and even toxic personalities in leadership positions, and some companies tolerate them more than others do. However, in organizations that are increasingly reliant on highly professional knowledge workers, extremely weak interpersonal skills are typically cast into high relief when someone is considered for promotion to the C-suite level. You are also unlikely to advance to the executive level if you hold a narrow, parochial perspective on the business and the organization. Such parochialism typically plays out in one of two ways: a selfish desire to see your unit succeed at the expense of other parts of the organization and a lack of understanding of how your decisions affect other parts of the company—for example, making a purely financial decision to improve profitability in the short term while ignoring the negative impact on the level of service provided to key customers.

The last deselection factor, putting self-interest above the company good, relates to a fine but important line. Those motivated to advance to the executive level are most often driven by a complex set of motives: a desire for power, prestige, financial gain, and sense of achievement. Most company's compensation programs are carefully crafted to stimulate a manager's performance and ambition. However, when you lose a sense of balance and put your personal agenda above the best interests of the organization, your credibility deteriorates, and the seeds of an ethical issue are sown. For example, if you are seen as shading information to look good in your current job, this creates a red flag for senior-level decision makers concerned about a more serious ethical breach should you advance to a position of greater authority and control of resources.

But the fact that you, a potential candidate, have all of the nonnegotiables and none of the deselection factors doesn't ensure success either. In most companies that is considered table stakes—the required minimum to be in the game. At this point six core selection factors come into play:

- *Demonstrating strategic skills:* the ability to generate winning strategies, create a sense of direction for the organization, and engage others behind that vision of the future

- *Building a strong management team:* the ability to identify and attract talent and create an adequate level of team cohesion

- *Managing implementation:* the ability to move from strategy to execution without being pulled too deeply into the details of implementation

- *Exhibiting the capacity for innovation and change:* the ability to depart from the status quo and lead large-scale change when circumstances require it

- *Working across organizational boundaries:* the ability to work with and through others across the company to get things done

- *Projecting executive presence:* the ability to establish your credibility as a leader quickly

These factors represent the five fundamental leadership tasks of the executive and a sixth capability, projecting executive presence, that are imperative for a senior leader to lead effectively at the executive level. These are the factors that in most companies determine whether you will or will not succeed in advancing to the executive level. Table 1.1 summarizes these unwritten rules.

In order to advance to the executive level, you need to demonstrate the core selection factors and nonnegotiables to senior-level decision makers while avoiding the deselection factors that will knock you out of the running. Those who make the ultimate decisions must clearly see in you the capabilities critical to advancement so they can feel comfortable about your ability to succeed as an executive. It is not enough for you to possess these abilities or for your boss to vouch for them to others. They must be seen and acknowledged by the key decision makers.

Table 1.1 The Unwritten Rules: Key Factors in Executive Career Advancement

Core selection factors: Most critical abilities in executive selection	Demonstrated ability to
	Think strategically: generate winning strategies; establish a sense of direction; engage others behind a vision of the future
	Build a strong management team: identify and attract talent; establish an adequate level of team cohesion
	Manage implementation: ensure predictable implementation of priorities and initiatives—without undue involvement at too low a level of detail
	Create the capacity for innovation and change: depart from the status quo; manage change
	Work across organizational boundaries to get things done (lateral management)
	Project executive presence: establish credibility as a leader quickly
Deselection factors: Characteristics that prevent one from being considered as a serious candidate	Weak interpersonal skills
	Insensitivity, abrasiveness
	Putting self-interest above the company good
	Narrow, parochial perspective on the business and organization
Nonnegotiables: Foundation factors for any candidate to be considered for an executive position	Consistent track record of performance and results
	Ethics, integrity, character
	Drive to lead; to assume higher levels of responsibility

YOUR CHALLENGE

For those of you who, like Mike Peterson, aspire to move up in the organization, the challenge starts with taking steps to understand the unwritten rules of advancement within your organization. Based on my experience and recent conversations with the HR heads at a number of large companies, the nonnegotiables and deselection factors are pretty universal. In all likelihood most, if not all, of my six core selection factors apply to your organization, but you may find one or two selection factors that are different due to the particular nature of your industry or your company's history.

A parallel challenge is to tease out from others where you stand in terms of those factors: what capabilities are viewed as your strengths and which you need to develop and display to the satisfaction of your company's key senior-level decision makers. Given that senior leaders typically have an aversion to providing this kind of feedback, you'll need to take the initiative to find out what people at senior levels think of you. In a persistent yet effective way, as described in the next chapter, you need to discover the deep-seated set of perceptions that superiors in your company have about your skills, experience, and leadership style. Right or wrong, this set of perceptions strongly affects how you are viewed in the organization and the kinds of positions you will be offered.

In this book, I strip away the curtain that in most companies obscures the reasons that aspiring executives like you do and do not advance to the executive level. I identify the skills and capabilities you need to develop and demonstrate in order to reach that level. In doing so, my objectives are fourfold:

1. To equip you to develop and display the key capabilities most often required for advancement to the executive level

2. To help you cut through the vague and unconstructive feedback you may receive in order to ferret out the deeply seated perceptions others have of your leadership abilities

3. To encourage organizations to be more explicit about the factors that are truly critical in determining promotions to the executive level—because otherwise you are pretty much in the dark about what's most important for you to work on developmentally

4. To encourage you and other managers in your company to have more candid and probing career discussions with your direct reports and to provide pivotal feedback about how your people are perceived within the organization, especially if those perceptions undermine executive decision makers' confidence in their ability to succeed at higher levels

In Chapter Two, I explore the obstacles you face in getting the candid feedback you need and the techniques you can employ to dig beneath vague or superficial comments to stimulate the "feedback that really counts." In Chapters Three through Eight, I delve into each of the six core selection factors, first defining each factor in specific terms and then highlighting what you can do to develop and demonstrate the required capability to others. Throughout I share the stories of managers I've assessed, coached, or observed directly. Some were successful in sharpening their leadership capabilities. Others struggled and failed to achieve their career goals, a fate I try to help you avoid.

In Chapters Nine and Ten, I offer you additional guidance on managing your career and preparing for success at the executive level. Finally, I conclude with a look at what managers—including you when you find yourself in the position to supervise a group of employees—can do to make the unwritten rules more explicit and, in the process, achieve a win-win outcome: a win for aspiring managers who will be able to exert greater control over their careers and a win for companies interested in finding productive ways to build executive talent while at the same time reducing unwanted attrition.

The journey I'm proposing for you isn't always easy. Teasing out where you stand in terms of your organization's unwritten rules typically requires some skill and creativity. Harder still can be responding to feedback that may seem inaccurate, unfair, or arbitrary to you. However, being armed with an accurate sense of how you are viewed by those who make executive placement decisions has one important benefit: it puts you in a position to take greater control of your career success and change the perceptions of others to your advantage. And that's my hope for you.

CHAPTER 2

The Feedback That Really Counts

Managers in most organizations get lots of feedback: whether you made your numbers; how you did in managing a project; whether you accomplished your annual performance goals. What you all too frequently miss is what I call the feedback that really counts—feedback about where you stand in terms of the unwritten rules governing who gets promoted to the executive level in your organization. According to the head of succession planning and management development of a well-known global financial firm, "Our executives often have great discussions about a potential leader within the company. The only problem is that the person is rarely in the room when they talk." Since most companies tend to do an extremely poor job of providing the feedback that really counts, it is often left up to you to tease out how senior-level decision makers perceive you, the initial step toward displaying the skills and behaviors required for success at higher levels.

But first, it's important to understand the reasons that executives in most organizations are hesitant to provide this kind of feedback and let people know where they stand in relation to their company's requirements for selection to the executive level. This understanding is critical as you prepare to take the initiative in soliciting candid and useful feedback. Several factors are in play that together inhibit most executives from providing meaningful feedback:

- *The inherent subjectivity of this kind of feedback.* The evaluation of your leadership style and skills tends to be highly subjective—in contrast to quantitative results, such as budget performance, that are easier for executives to specify and discuss. Skills like "strategic thinking" and "leading innovation" are critical to success at the executive level, but they are also subject to different definitions and standards. Executives' perceptions of your capabilities are typically the result of direct experience with you and comments that others make over a period of time. For example, how you field a question during a presentation to a senior executive group can influence opinions about your level of self-confidence and ability to handle pressure. A trusted member of an executive's staff may have expressed frustration with how you dealt with a conflict situation and complained that you are not a team player. Over months and years, such comments and direct experience come together to create a "gut feel" within the senior leader, and the incidents or comments that combined to create that sense may have faded from memory. Executives often struggle to articulate the intuitive, almost visceral feelings that stand in the way of their sense of confidence that an individual can succeed at higher levels. As a result, they tend to hold back on providing direct feedback, especially when that feedback is hard to substantiate in an objective way.

• *Obstacles in most companies to achieving a consensus point of view of a manager's leadership skills and career potential.* The opinions executives have of a particular manager can vary significantly based on their positions within the organization and the degree of contact they have had with the person. In most organizations, it's hard to find time to bring members of the executive team together for a balanced, probing discussion of a candidate for promotion in order to sort through everyone's perspectives and come to agreement about the candidate's strengths, development needs, and career potential. In the absence of such a consensus, many executives are leery of being out of step with others on the leadership team in their views of the candidate, another reason for holding back on feedback.

• *A desire not to demotivate a manager who receives less-than-glowing feedback* or fear of creating unwanted attrition on the part of strong performers who are not seen as promotable to the next level.

• *A tendency to jump to the conclusion that a manager is incapable of developing some needed skill.* When senior executives have reached this conclusion, they fear that delivering feedback will be counterproductive and only frustrate the manager. In reality, some executive-level capabilities are extremely difficult to develop. However, in the absence of candid and constructive feedback, the likelihood that a manager will develop or display a required capability is virtually nil.

These four reasons combine with the very human tendency to avoid giving people bad news, hurting their feelings, and possibly prompting a negative emotional response. Imagine that a senior executive's lack of confidence in a manager's ability to succeed at higher levels is based on a "gut feel" that she cannot fully articulate. In the absence of a well-defined consensus involving other senior executives about the manager's abilities and career potential, she will shy away from direct and candid feedback, especially when she cannot defend her intuitive sense with facts or specific examples of the manager's lack of ability. When pressed by the aspiring manager for an explanation of why he didn't get promoted, it's almost always safer for the senior executive to move the conversation to more neutral territory, for example, the job experience the manager hasn't had, the projects he needs to complete, or the results she would like to see him produce. For all of these reasons, an upwardly aspiring manager who has not received quality feedback needs to be skilled in finding ways to access the feedback that really counts.

Since so many executives are reluctant to provide direct feedback to upwardly aspiring managers, a number of companies rely on 360-degree surveys to fill this feedback gap. A 360-degree survey involves asking your boss, peers, direct reports, and other coworkers to complete confidential surveys that rate you on a range of leadership skills. Once completed, the surveys are consolidated to ensure anonymity before the results are shared with you. Often the surveys are based on the company's leadership model, comprising a number of management skills the company looks for in its managers and executives. Examples include things like "displays a sense of urgency," "anticipates and responds to the needs of customers," "works well with others across the organization," and "treats others fairly and with respect." Although 360-degree feedback surveys are a relatively inexpensive way to provide general developmental feedback, they are rarely effective as a stand-alone tool in getting at the feedback that really counts, for three main reasons:

1. They usually focus on the broad range of leadership skills included in a company's leadership model—as opposed to the most critical factors that senior-level decision makers consider in making executive-level promotional decisions.

2. They evaluate a manager's strengths and development needs in her current position—as opposed to the skills required for success at higher levels. As an example, it is often difficult to evaluate a manager's delegation abilities when she is a hands-on manager of a small, highly technical group working closely with her direct reports. Highly refined delegation skills are not terribly important at her current level, but they would become critical if she was asked to lead a much bigger organization.

3. They often miss important contextual factors within the organization that surround a manager. Given the stresses and strains organizations create, perceptions about a manager's development needs can become intertwined and magnified in unexpected ways, as the story of Tom Chambers illustrates.

For many years, Tom had enjoyed a highly successful career with the Specialty Financial Company, a high-quality, relatively slow-moving firm that put a high value on technical proficiency and customer service. Tom had been a member of a stable management team for several years and was highly regarded throughout the company. Then things suddenly changed. The company's parent corporation decided to bring in a new CEO to capitalize on perceived marketplace opportunities. Shortly after, Tom's manager retired after a long career with the company and was replaced by a senior executive from another division within the parent corporation. Tom's new boss's management approach was based on speed and the ability to produce results quickly, and she came into her new job with a well-defined agenda for growing the business.

Six months after Tom's new boss joined the team, concerns about Tom's performance began to surface within the company. Long-term colleagues who had always known Tom as a team player and straight shooter began to describe him as difficult to work with. Tom's direct reports still enjoyed working for him, but they described him as being distracted at times and on edge. Given Tom's past record of top-notch performance and the company's desire to retain an acknowledged technical expert, the company asked me to work with Tom to rectify the situation. Since I had been involved with the company for a number of years and knew its leaders well, I understood the business and cultural sea-change that was occurring at Specialty Financial.

To get started, I suggested that Tom conduct a 360-degree feedback survey based on Specialty Financial's leadership model. The survey included a range of questions that invited others to rate Tom's business acumen, strategic vision, customer focus, collaboration, people development skills, and so forth. In addition to the survey, I recommended engaging in a series of confidential interviews with Tom's new boss and a number of Tom's peers and direct reports. I also arranged to meet with Tom to get a sense of how he was responding to the new company direction and leadership approach.

The results of the 360-degree survey showed that Tom was well regarded for his business knowledge, technical skills, customer focus, and commitment to the best interests of the company. The survey also indicated two major areas that needed attention on Tom's part: (1) devoting additional time to his working relationships with his peers and (2) increasing his level of comfort in making decisions faster. This was all useful stuff, but the survey findings did not get to the core, let alone severity, of Tom's issues. The results of the confidential interviews I conducted clearly indicated that Tom's level of trust with his peers and coworkers was rapidly eroding. When presented with this feedback, Tom was thunderstruck. He considered himself highly ethical and couldn't understand how his peers, many of whom he had worked with for years, could ever doubt his integrity.

The interviews had revealed how certain aspects of Tom's personality and leadership style were playing out in the context of the changes within the company. According to his peers, Tom would frequently set up meetings to discuss a proposed new initiative that he and his manager were advocating. When his peers voiced skepticism or raised concerns about the proposal, Tom became quiet and unresponsive, and they assumed he agreed with their position—even though he never clearly stated his opinion one way or the other. Although he appeared on the surface to be seeking their thoughts on the proposed initiative, his peers never felt that he acknowledged or addressed their concerns in any real way. In several instances, they later heard through others within the company that the initiative Tom had come to discuss was being pushed ahead without their concurrence. As a result, they felt they were now seeing a side of Tom quite different from what they had experienced in the past: a noncollaborative tendency to end-run his peers to get what he wanted.

When I provided him with this feedback, Tom acknowledged that he was feeling pressured by his new boss and the less-than-collegial environment ushered in by the company's new leadership team. His new boss wanted results fast and was prepared to move ahead even if there was some resistance on the part of Tom's peers. Tom confessed that he was anxious about his ability to produce results quickly enough for his manager. In addition, he explained that he had never felt entirely comfortable with conflict, especially if it was accompanied by strong emotions and when he didn't have enough time to fully research the issue at hand. In such situations he tended to freeze and withdraw from the conversation, his face becoming impassive and hard for others to read. Given his lack of comfort with conflict, he was more likely to remain silent than disagree openly with peers when they challenged him. As we talked, he began to understand that others interpreted his silence as assent—even if that wasn't what he intended—and how his actions were contributing to a trust issue.

Based on the feedback from my interviews, Tom began to realize that he needed to learn how to handle conflict with peers in a more open and above-board manner—even if he was forced to agree to disagree with them. Otherwise his peers' concerns about his trustworthiness would hijack his credibility and create an obstacle to his remaining with the company, let alone future advancement. In the course of continued coaching, Tom also learned that although he was respected for his technical skills and industry experience, his cautious and overly analytical approach was increasingly viewed as signaling resistance to change. In essence, the same qualities that had been highly valued in the past were now seen as at odds with the business strategy and leadership approach recently introduced within the company.

Being a highly analytical type, Tom scoured his 360-degree feedback results to compare them to the summary of the confidential interviews I provided. Although his feedback report hinted at the underlying issues, he came to understand that the survey results did not show the relationship among the various pieces of the equation that emerged in the course of the confidential interviews. In the context of a new business strategy emphasizing speed of action and decision making, a new leadership team prepared to accept a greater degree of conflict than before, and the demands of his new manager, Tom's behavior, especially his response to challenge, was being interpreted in ways vastly different from what he intended. Armed with a better sense of how he was being perceived by others, Tom began to work on being more open and demonstrative with his colleagues. That included being clear about when he agreed with them and when he didn't. He started to engage in more explicit dialogue with his boss to understand which aspects of new initiatives were open to debate and which he and his peers needed to accept as proposed. By taking these steps, he was largely successful in addressing the issue of trust that had surfaced in the confidential interviews.

Tom was fortunate that his company had invested in getting him an external coach who, through the confidential interviews, was able to zero in on vital feedback not forthcoming from other sources, including the 360-degree feedback survey. More often, though, aspiring executives must take the initiative to solicit feedback themselves in order to know what skills and abilities they need to develop and demonstrate in order to change widely held perceptions that can hold them back. In order to do so successfully, you'll need to answer three important questions: who to ask, how to ask, and how to respond.

WHO TO ASK

Your current manager is an obvious starting point for getting feedback. Regardless of the nature of your working relationship or how long you have reported to him, begin your conversations with your boss. If he's candid, his feedback will be useful since he is typically the one closest to your work and his perspectives can shape the opinions of senior executives. Realize, however, that your manager may not be willing to give you the straight scoop (especially if there are concerns about retaining or demotivating you) and that his views about your career potential and most important development issues may be different from those of other key decision makers. In any case, your boss will almost certainly be involved if you choose to contact others for their input since senior executives will usually ask for a green light from your boss before agreeing to speak with you.

Clearly there are others in the organization you should approach for feedback. As a rule of thumb, try to contact the highest-level managers who are knowledgeable about your work and with whom you've had a positive working relationship so that your approach for feedback seems natural and appropriate. For example, try to approach your former manager or your boss's boss—assuming you have had interaction with her—or the leader of another group you have worked closely with. Ensure that you inform your current manager about any contact you have with other executives regarding such discussions so she doesn't misinterpret your motives.

Make sure that the executives you approach understand clearly why you are seeking their input: to gain additional insight into your career development priorities. Try to space these conversations out over a number of weeks or even months so that you don't appear to be simply lobbying for a promotion. It's likely that you will hear somewhat different messages about how you are perceived from different individuals. That's typical since each executive will have had distinct interactions with you and will likely prioritize your key areas of development differently depending on his or her experience and role within the organization. For example, an executive who once ran the international sales group—and considers that job his most useful learning experience—may say that you need global exposure, while an executive in charge of a large business unit may feel strongly that you need to work on strategic thinking or managing implementation—skills critical in her current job. Look hard for the patterns and commonalities that emerge from your conversations, especially if they relate to the core selection factors described in this book. Most likely they are the fundamental outline of how you are perceived within the organization.

For the reasons I've already described in this chapter, some people may feel uncomfortable giving you direct feedback. Nevertheless, they may still serve as good sounding boards to test the conclusions you draw from your conversations with others. For example, in some organizations senior-level HR staff sit in on staffing or succession planning meetings. Often an HR executive is reluctant to share directly feedback gained from those closed-door conversations for fear of broaching confidential information. However, she may respond if you share the feedback you've received from other executives and let you know if you are hearing the right messages.

HOW TO ASK

If there was ever a time for active listening, this is it. When you ask an executive for feedback, it is vital to project a sincere desire to understand how you are perceived and the skills and capabilities you need to demonstrate in order to advance your career. Avoid any tendency to argue a point of feedback. Anything you say that conveys defensiveness or any negative body language is likely to reinforce the other person's inhibitions and cause him to either shut down or move the conversation to safer, but less productive, territory. Instead, ask clarifying questions or request examples that illustrate the feedback, but stay clear of comments that appear to challenge the feedback or attempt to change the person's mind. If you find that erroneous information has created a false perception on the part of the other person (for example, that you unnecessarily delayed a major project when in fact the project team decided as a whole to extend the project timetable in order to complete some important research), file that away and deal with it later. Don't allow your efforts to correct the matter on the spot to be seen as defensiveness.

Sometimes you'll receive feedback phrased in overly general terms such as a need for "better communication skills" or "increased leadership." Such comments are usually code words for important issues. Continue to ask probing questions in an attempt to get behind the other person's comments and ferret out the underlying skills and capabilities they feel you are missing or need to demonstrate. For example, if you hear you need to gain more "managerial experience" in your current role, this may indicate a perceived need to build a stronger management team or to drive organizational change. Becoming a "more impactful team player" may signal that you need to develop your skills in influence, persuasion, and collaborative problem solving as well as your political savvy: knowing how to influence key decision makers to get your proposals accepted at higher levels within the company. When it comes to style or behavioral issues—the kind that executives are often most uncomfortable discussing—try to get the person to describe what success looks like. For example, if an executive suggests that you improve your "communication" skills, ask, "What would people see if I improved my communication skills?" A clearer, more succinct verbal style? Better presentation skills? Taking the time to allow others to express themselves? Being more open to what others have to say? Your request that they describe success often makes it easier for executives to identify issues they are struggling to define or articulate.

An open, candid feedback discussion can begin to paint a clear picture of how you are perceived within the organization and your opportunities for growth. At the end of a productive feedback session, try to get a sense of the person's opinion about the skills he feels you ought to focus on developing or demonstrating the most. Ask one important summary question: "What one or two things—above all others—would most help build others' confidence in my ability to succeed at higher levels within the organization at some point in the future?" Assuming that the other person has leveled with you during the conversation, this question tends to get to the core issues of how you are perceived within the organization and what you need to display in order to move ahead.

HOW TO RESPOND

If you've been successful in determining how you are truly perceived within the organization, the results can unleash strong emotions. Learning that senior executives, some of whom may know you only superficially, have significant questions or concerns about your leadership capabilities is not easy. Your first response may be that the feedback is inaccurate or unfair or that you're the victim of a double standard since you know of others who have been promoted without the skills you are seen as lacking. These are some of the common reactions I hear from my clients:

- "How can I be accused of not being an innovative or strategic thinker when the company has never encouraged that? The culture has always rewarded implementers and those who can make their numbers. Since when has strategic thinking become such a big deal?"

- "The new management team has moved the goalposts about what they want leaders to do. How can those of us who grew up in the company have a chance to succeed when senior management keeps changing direction about what it expects of leaders?"

- "I've seen other people promoted without this or that skill. Why are they making it such an issue with me?"

- "How can someone be a team player when our senior executives are engaged in turf wars? How can I be collaborative with my peers when all they do is push their own agendas and refuse to compromise?"

- "Developing talent makes sense in theory, but the HR department won't let me deal with performance problems on my staff. I know what needs to be done, but the system won't let me do it."

The first step in responding to the feedback you've received, often after calming down and letting the dust settle a bit, is to face a basic fact: right or wrong, how you are perceived has a huge impact on whether you'll get promoted to the C-suite level. Your actions over time and in the context of your organization's culture have combined to create a widespread sense of your leadership skills and capabilities. In the course of my career, I've worked with managers who have complained that no one in the company ever leveled with them about the feedback that really counts. In many cases, they were right. But in some cases, others in the organization tried to convey that feedback, without success. Maybe it could have been provided more clearly or directly, but there's a human tendency to not hear what you don't want to hear. So if you do succeed in teasing out this kind of feedback, it's up to you to make sense out of what you hear and act on it. Simply bemoaning what you see as unfair feedback will ultimately get in the way of your efforts to change how you are perceived to your advantage.

As a next step, carefully prioritize the information you've received, and try to identify the one or two things you need to demonstrate in a consistent way in order to change the commonly held perceptions that are holding you back. In doing so, I suggest you refer to the nonnegotiables, deselection factors, and core selection factors highlighted in Chapter One so you choose the most important issues and avoid focusing on minor ones. Keep in mind that you don't need to be perfect as a leader, and you don't have to win the support of every senior executive in the company. You simply need to change the perceptions of certain senior executives—those likely to be influential in making decisions about the positions you'd like to move up to, so that in their minds, any potential concerns have been neutralized.

Next, answer the following question as precisely as you can: "How would I like people to describe me differently in six to nine months?" More innovative? More open to new ideas? More forward looking and focused on the marketplace? More comfortable with uncertainty and taking risks? Able to let go of certain details while still making sure work gets done? As you think through the feedback you've received, make sure that you frame your response to this question in a way that is clear and meaningful to you.

Finally, identify specific opportunities in your job to demonstrate the new skill you've identified. The following chapters provide specific suggestions about how to develop and demonstrate the core selection factors outlined in Chapter One. Be aware that you won't fundamentally change perceptions unless others can see you doing something new and then share their observations with others within the organization. In some cases, you may find that the nature of your position prevents you from demonstrating a particular skill. For example, your unit may be pretty well self-contained, with few opportunities to work across organizational lines with other groups. Similarly, your role may be devoted to implementing preestablished strategies, making it hard to display your strategic abilities. If that's the case, you may need to engineer a move to a new assignment, where it is easier to demonstrate the desired capability. More often than not, however, you are likely to find opportunities to display required skills in your current role. For example, with your boss's help, you can get named to a company-wide project where you can broaden your perspective and showcase your skills in influencing and persuading others.

As you begin working to demonstrate new skills, keep one important point in mind: changing deeply held perceptions on the part of people within an organization takes time and persistence. Others may not notice subtle changes. Also, if you are inconsistent in your behavior and occasionally revert to your old ways, you'll undermine your efforts to change others' perceptions of you. Keep your sights tightly focused on the one to two priority capabilities you have identified. Make sure that you work to display new skills in a continuous way that is highly visible so others can see that you're operating in a new mode.

In reality, deeply held perceptions can occasionally be so strong and so negative that it is virtually impossible to change them, even with your best efforts. If this is your situation, it may be necessary for you to leave the company and create a new set of perceptions of your leadership skills elsewhere. Remember, though, that serious leadership deficiencies displayed in one company are likely to crop up in a new organization without significant and sustained effort on your part to change them. All things being equal, it's easier and preferable to try to build a new skill in a company where you know the people and the business than it is in a new company where much of your effort must be devoted to learning the ropes and creating a reputation as someone able to produce results.

In most organizations, successfully teasing out the feedback that really counts—feedback about what is central to your ability to move ahead—is tough enough. But armed with accurate feedback, the hard work of development begins. In the next six chapters, we'll explore the six core selection factors most companies use to make executive-level, C-suite placement decisions. After defining these factors, I identify the most critical questions aspiring executives must answer in the affirmative to instill confidence on the part of senior-level decision makers. Then I describe the actions you can take to build your reputation for possessing that skill.

Time to get started.

CHAPTER 3

FACTOR 1
Demonstrating Strategic Skills

I n the course of my work, I often ask senior executives to define *leadership* and the skills they look for in their companies' leaders. Although phrased in somewhat different terms, the responses from virtually all senior executives quickly point to two critical skills: the ability to create a strategy that helps the business succeed over the long run and the ability to motivate the organization to follow that strategic direction. These answers aren't surprising since devising strategy and setting the course for the organization is an executive's most fundamental task, while inspiring others to follow a new direction has been the essence of leadership from time immemorial.

For many managers who aspire to crack the C-suite level, the requirement that they demonstrate strategic skills and impart a sense of direction to the organization often presents a serious dilemma. Managers complain, and rightly so, that only high-level executives are called on to create strategy in their organizations. So how do you display what I call your "strategic gears" if devising strategy is not typically expected of someone at your level? The requirement that future executives demonstrate strategic thinking ability is complicated by the fact that members of your company's senior executive team may define *strategy* in different terms. Depending on the executive, *strategy* can mean corporate strategy, strategy for an operating group or division, or strategy for a functional department like finance or information technology.[1] So what are senior-level decision makers looking for, and how do you demonstrate it to their satisfaction?

To cut through such dilemmas, I encourage you to focus on the key questions you need to answer in the minds of key decision makers and the skills you need to demonstrate to their satisfaction. Regardless of how they define *strategy*, those who make promotional decisions to the executive level typically look for definitive answers to the following questions. Can this individual

- Establish and maintain a consistent set of priorities—as opposed to chasing the initiative of the day?

- Think in a big-picture, long-term way—as opposed to focusing exclusively on short-term results or a narrow slice of the business?

- Anticipate and respond to marketplace trends that are critical to the company's future success?

- Generate or lead the creation of a new, winning strategy—as opposed to skillfully implementing a strategy that someone else developed?

- Convey a strategic vision in a way that inspires and motivates the organization to act?

In order to answer these questions in the affirmative, you need to put yourself in a position to display a number of abilities to the key decision makers. These skills include abstract and conceptual thinking ability and the ability to translate often complex strategic concepts into a series of coherent messages and communicate them in a way that excites people at various levels within the organization.

In this chapter, I offer suggestions on how you can develop and display your strategic thinking skills to their fullest, as well as how to navigate your way through a career management dilemma some managers encounter. But I have one caveat: the abstract thinking and conceptual skills involved in strategic thinking are not easy to develop. They relate to innate abilities such as the ability to see patterns that aren't obvious to most people, connect information from a variety of sources in creative ways, and spot trends and anticipate where they are likely to lead. Such skills are usually hard-wired by the time people become adults—if not before. In the course of this chapter, I will, however, offer some tips on how you can compensate if operating on a strategic plane doesn't come easily to you and how to showcase the strategic abilities you do have.

To set the stage for that, let me introduce you to Mary Thompson and Phil Whalen, two managers I had a chance to work with over a period of time. As you'll see, Mary had natural strategic ability, but she still worked hard to maximize her skills. Phil did many of the right things, but in the end he came up short in engaging people to support a new strategic direction.

Mary Thompson

When I first met Mary Thompson, she was already a rising star within her company, a consumer products giant, and in the process of building her reputation as a highly strategic and visionary leader. It was fascinating to watch her career progress over the next several years and the steps she took to develop her innate strategic ability. Mary was extremely bright and blessed with excellent conceptual ability. Highly analytical by nature, she could see the big picture and was good at spotting trends. She was also articulate and a terrific presenter. And beyond that, she was able to convey her views with tremendous conviction. Although Mary was warm and personable, her tenacity was clearly evident when she spoke.

Mary's career path within the company was unusual in many respects, but the experience she gained along the way served her well. She had joined the company immediately after completing her M.B.A. She spent several years in the corporate finance department analyzing major expenditures, potential investments, and competitive activity on behalf of the company. This experience helped her understand the factors that drove the company's profitability and stock price. She also learned the industry forces that influenced the marketplace and how the company's key competitors operated.

Although Mary was successful in her corporate finance role, she yearned to be closer to the business. Using her expanding network among the company's finance managers, she engineered a move into a finance role within one of the company's business units. Once in her new job, she was able to contribute immediately by employing her financial and analytical skills. Not content to play a purely internal role, she petitioned her new boss and several leaders in the business unit to allow her to visit the group's field operations and attend customer meetings. In the process, she built strong relationships with several sales managers in the field, people she later relied on to provide her with information about marketplace activities.

After a few years as business unit financial manager, her career within the company began to take off. She had become well versed in the needs of the unit's key customers. In addition, she became aware of the trend toward consolidation within the industry and the growing power of the company's large customers. As her industry knowledge grew, she was asked to coordinate the business unit's annual strategic planning process. Shortly after, she became one of the key architects of the unit's new strategy, one that centered on meeting the needs of several large, important customers. Given her strong communication skills and ability to explain the financial impact of the unit's new strategy, Mary was asked to join the team that presented the strategy to the company's senior leadership team, earning rave reviews in the process. She was also highly successful in building support for the new strategy within the business unit organization. Those who attended the employee meetings Mary conducted throughout the business unit came away impressed by her ability to communicate the new strategy to the troops in a highly motivational way.

Not long afterward, the company underwent a major reorganization. With her reputation as a strategic, visionary leader well established, it came as no surprise when Mary was named to a key position on the corporation's new executive team.

Phil Whalen

Phil Whalen was group director of human resources (HR) for the biggest business unit of a large high-tech company, and he was responsible for a team of HR professionals. When I first met Phil, he had received some important feedback from his boss, the business unit president and from the corporate head of HR. Some concerns had also been expressed by members of his team. In a nutshell, the feedback Phil received indicated that he was seen as a highly capable HR manager whom leaders and employees throughout the business unit could rely on for sound advice on any personnel-related matter. The business unit president, however, didn't think that Phil had been successful in anticipating the organizational and HR requirements of the unit's new strategic plan. In addition, some of his staff members complained that the department didn't have a unifying strategy and that priorities within the group shifted too much—a phenomenon they called the "priority du jour."

In response to this feedback, Phil enlisted his team of direct reports in a textbook example of strategic planning for a staff support group such as HR. He and his team members fanned out and interviewed each of the unit's senior leaders to get a sense of their business priorities and HR needs. He asked members of his team to collect data about the marketplace changes likely to influence the future supply and cost of employing staff, and they researched employment-related regulations that might affect the company in the future.

Phil then scheduled a series of strategic planning sessions with his team. During those meetings, they thoughtfully reviewed the data collected and considered what the unit's executives had said about their HR needs. The team spent a great deal of time clarifying its mission and value proposition: the key services they would offer their internal customers in a consistent, high-quality way. As the planning effort progressed, the members of Phil's team began to line up behind the new HR strategy and priorities that emerged. As they prepared to communicate their new plan, there was real enthusiasm within the team about the new direction they had created together. Then things stalled badly.

Phil was responsible for one key part of the team's communication plan: presenting the new HR strategy to the business unit's leadership team to get their support. But Phil was not completely sure he could sell the plan to his boss, the business unit president, and he felt gun-shy about pressing the issue with him. Phil tried to get time on the agenda of the business unit leadership team's monthly meeting, but the topic kept being preempted by more urgent issues. About this time, Phil and members of his team scheduled a meeting with their HR department staff to review the new strategy. When Phil spoke, the results were disappointing. Those in attendance described his presentation as a laundry list of priorities that were not connected by any larger sense of vision. Phil's delivery style was mechanical and uninspiring. Staff members who attended the presentation came away with major questions about Phil's commitment to driving the strategy within the business unit and getting the support necessary from the corporate HR department.

Phil's strategic planning effort, which had begun with great promise, soon fizzled out. A few new programs were successfully implemented, but the strategy was quickly forgotten. Phil continued to be viewed as a capable HR manager, and he provided high-quality support to a number of groups within the company over the ensuing years. However, he was never considered as a candidate for promotion to the next level. Questions lingered about his ability to engage with business executives on a strategic level and to unite an organization behind a new sense of direction.

CAN STRATEGIC THINKING ABILITY BE DEVELOPED?

Virtually every senior executive I speak with agrees that the ability to think strategically and create a sense of direction for an organization is a requirement for success at the executive level. Some, however, aren't convinced that strategic thinking is a skill that can be developed. My answer to that is yes—and no. It's true that strategic thinking comes more easily to some managers than others, and clearly not every manager possesses the strategic skills to become a CEO. However, there's a big difference between being blessed with natural strategic ability and having the knowledge, experience, and perspective to deploy it fully.

Ultimately your strategic skills will be evaluated based on your ability to lead the creation of a new strategy for your organization. In the process, you'll need to display the ability to generate strategic insight, translate your new strategy into a concrete set of priorities, and then unite your organization behind the new strategy. Your success in demonstrating these skills starts with devoting adequate time to strategic activities and taking the steps needed to establish your reputation as a leader who operates on a strategic plane.

GENERATING STRATEGIC INSIGHT

If you've received feedback about the need to develop and display your strategic skills, I suggest you turn to four strategies that collectively can help you leverage your inherent abilities.

Broaden Your Range of Strategic Inputs

Flexing your strategic muscles often begins with getting out to the marketplace and spending time with customers (who, depending on your role, may be external or internal to the company) to deepen your understanding of their needs. Many managers complain that they are too busy with the demands of their job to find time for visiting customers, meeting with people in a field office, or reading about industry trends. However, if you can't find ways to carve out time for such strategic activities at your current level, you're unlikely to be able to do so at a higher level given the increased pressures of more senior positions. In order to devote time to such activities, you may need to learn to delegate more effectively and improve your ability to oversee implementation of major initiatives in your area—at the same time you reduce your level of direct involvement. (This is a topic I come back to in Chapter Five.)

Recall how Mary Thompson, even when she was in a finance manager role, arranged to visit the field and attend customer meetings. These meetings gave her firsthand insight into customer needs and competitive activity. Over time she was able to build relationships with people in the sales organization who became her eyes and ears to help spot industry trends such as the growing power of major customers. Based on her expanded knowledge and relationships, people in her organization began to see her in a new light, and she was able to create new strategies that helped her unit succeed in the marketplace versus its competitors.

Make it a point, as Mary did, to increase your network of people within and outside your company who can feed your strategic intelligence. Ask them what sources of industry information they track. Whether it's joining industry associations, attending conferences on strategic topics, or reading marketplace updates, make keeping current with industry events part of your ongoing education.

Broaden Your Perspective on the Business and the Industry

As you seek to build your strategic thinking skills, consider whether the job experiences you've had have developed the breadth of perspective on the business and industry that's often required for strategic thinking. As an example, consider how Mary Thompson was able to navigate her career at her company. After a number of years in an internally focused staff role, she managed to orchestrate a variety of business unit assignments that gave her direct customer contact and a ringside seat on the marketplace. In all likelihood, Mary's inherent abstract thinking and conceptual abilities didn't change as she progressed through her different assignments. However, the increased perspective she gained along the way allowed her to think about the business in new ways, and she was able to develop her credibility as a strategist steeped in the realities of the business.

To truly expand your strategic thinking horizons, you may need to engineer a new set of job assignments that will broaden your perspective and allow you to see the business in more holistic ways. In the meantime, though, while you are still in your current job, try to get involved in cross-functional projects and teams—the kind that allow you to engage in a broader set of issues than you normally deal with and interact with people from other business units and functions in your company. The relationships you build will expand your ongoing network—one that can supply new insights to contribute to your strategic thinking.

Brush Up on Your Knowledge of Strategic Planning

Look for ways to jump-start your strategic thinking. What's your background in strategy, and how up-to-date

54

is it? A strategy course from business school ten or twenty years ago is probably not sufficient to provide you with the range of models and concepts required to engage your strategic gears. See if your company offers a course in strategic planning, or enroll in an external program where you can be introduced to new approaches to strategy. In external programs, you'll have a chance to work with managers from a variety of companies and industries and expand your network in the process.

As an alternative, locate a strategy coach inside or outside the organization—someone who can introduce you to useful strategy frameworks. An external coach may be a retired business executive who teaches at a local university. An internal coach is typically a highly strategic manager who will agree to meet with you periodically to discuss your company's strategic issues and opportunities. A seasoned external coach will provide guidance about how new strategy concepts can be applied to your organization. By contrast, the right internal coach can help equip you to engage with your boss and peers in generating new strategies to help your unit respond to marketplace change.

In addition to learning as much as you can about trends in your industry, expand your reading list to include books that describe how companies in other industries have addressed strategic issues. For example, what did Microsoft do in its early days to sow the seeds for its predominant market share? How did Starbucks transform a commodity product such as coffee into an international phenomenon? What allowed Dell to skyrocket to success—and what does it need to do now to recapture a dominant position in its industry? Often analogies from other companies in different industries can trigger new ways of thinking about strategy for your own business.

Let Others See and Hear You Engaging on Strategic Issues

When was the last time you initiated a long-term strategic planning effort within your organization? In most of the companies I work with, the so-called strategic or annual planning process is little more than a budgeting exercise. If your company's planning process doesn't stimulate a longer-term view of its strategic issues, I suggest that you strike out on your own. Work with members of your team, and use what you've learned about the marketplace, customer needs, and industry trends to organize your own strategic planning and priority-setting process. Doing so allows you and the members of your team to rise above day-to-day activities. Whether you manage a business unit or a functional department, you'll be more proactive in anticipating issues and putting in place strategies that strengthen your organization for the longer term. Assuming that the priorities that emerge from your work are grounded in a well-considered future strategy, you'll be armed to communicate a compelling vision to more senior managers and members of your organization.

As you take steps to establish your reputation as a strategic thinker, consider what people hear you talking about on a day-to-day basis. That by itself often plays a major part in shaping others' perceptions of your strategic skills. Some managers who have succeeded based on their ability to manage implementation focus the bulk of their attention and conversation on internal company activities, next-quarter business results, or the status of current initiatives. They often shoot down blue-sky thinking on the part of others or are too quick to challenge the practicality of new ideas that others propose. These reactions tend to dampen the flow of strategic discussions while reinforcing their reputation for excessive emphasis on the short term and the tactical. By contrast, let others hear you talking about marketplace events, competitive activity, future possibilities, and contingencies. When you engage in the kinds of strategic activities and discussions I've described, you will be reinforcing your image as a strategic thinker, and over time senior executives in your company will take notice.

STRENGTHENING YOUR ABILITY TO COMMUNICATE A STRATEGIC VISION

Note that one of the key questions that decision makers consider when it comes to your strategic ability is, "Can this person convey a strategic vision in a way that inspires and motivates the organization to act?" At the executive level, the ability to convey a new strategy in a way that energizes and guides the organization requires sophisticated communication skills. Assuming you and your team have been successful in crafting a winning strategy and set of priorities, your next step becomes employing your communication skills, especially your ability to transform often complex strategic concepts into a compelling sense of vision and articulate that vision in a way that excites others.

Fortunately, many managers find it easier to develop communication and public speaking skills than strategic ones. Public speaking courses and coaches can help develop your ability to speak confidently to large groups. In addition to formal training, identify opportunities to observe those who are effective in communicating with people at different organizational levels. Watch executives within the company, as well as leaders in virtually any other field, who have been successful in motivating others when they speak. Almost always, such speakers have developed the ability to tailor their approach to the audience: to vary their style based on the interests of the audience and speak in terms that are meaningful to them.

Most senior management groups tend to like presentations in which key strategies and tactics are spelled out clearly and supported by relevant data. By contrast, in communicating a new strategy to an employee group, avoid the tendency to overkill a presentation with data and detail. Instead find the anecdotes and images that speak to what members of the audience value most. As an example, one general manager I've worked with leads a business unit at a large health care company. In employee meetings, he focuses his strategy updates on how the business unit is contributing to the company's mission of improving the health of people around the world and increasing the efficiency of the overall health care system.

When called on to communicate a new strategy, some managers never feel comfortable in front of a large group—even after having invested in coaching and training to increase their public speaking skills. If that's you, I suggest that you change the venue. Think about the settings where you feel most comfortable communicating with others, for example, small group meetings with fifteen to twenty staff members, informal brown bag lunches with employees, or attending a direct report's staff meeting with her team. Once you've identified the venue that works well for you, find someone knowledgeable about the interests and concerns of the group you'll be meeting with—someone who can help you shape your message and approach to the audience.

Regardless of your audience, make sure that you successfully convey your personal commitment to the strategies and priorities established. Some people, like Mary Thompson, are good cheerleaders, and some leaders are more low-key in their presentation approach. Whatever your style, make sure your personal conviction and commitment are visible, and avoid dry, data-driven presentations that can prevent your conviction from coming through.

COMPENSATING FOR LESS-THAN-STELLAR STRATEGIC ABILITIES

Strategic thinking is probably the hardest of the core selection factors to develop given the requirement for a high level of abstract thinking and conceptual ability. As a result, leaders who aspire to the executive level may need to consider ways to compensate for their natural abilities if strategic thinking doesn't come easily.

Some years ago I had a chance to observe Pete Bianchi when he took over as the general manager of a business unit at a large consumer products company. He had been selected for the GM role because the unit relied on its success in selling to large, well-established customers—and Pete, who had begun his career in sales, had a reputation as a strong, results-oriented sales manager who was highly skilled in dealing with customers. Prior to taking on his GM role, Pete had received feedback that some senior executives within the company questioned his strategic thinking abilities. So it was interesting to see how Pete went about setting a new strategic direction for his business unit as he moved into his new job.

Soon after taking over as GM, Pete brought on to his team two direct reports who were known for their strategic thinking abilities. He then decided to update the unit's strategic plan. The approach included a series of management team off-site meetings aimed at generating a new strategy and getting Pete's team members lined up behind it. At these team planning sessions, Pete played an effective facilitator role. Although he wasn't the source of any breakthrough ideas, he led the team's discussions and encouraged blue-sky thinking on the part of team members. Given his knowledge of the marketplace, he provided insight into competitors' strategies and helped the team think through how competitors were likely to respond to the strategies under consideration.

Once the team had developed its new strategy and related business priorities, Pete began to employ his excellent communication skills. He reviewed the new strategy with the company's senior leadership team and scheduled several all-employee meetings within the business unit to build support for the new strategy. A born salesman who had presided over numerous sales conventions in the course of his career, he was in his element during the all-employee meetings. He asked several of his direct reports to present different parts of the new strategic plan. However, Pete kicked off each meeting and brought the session to a close, so there was no question in the minds of the unit's staff that Pete owned the plan. These meetings resulted in a strong buzz throughout the organization and real sign-up for the strategy and the priorities Pete and his team members had created.

In truth, Pete didn't possess outstanding strategic skills, and that continued to be evident to the corporation's senior executives. However, he was successful in compensating for his shortcomings up to a point. Although he never rose to the company's executive ranks due to concerns about his strategic skills, he was successful in several GM positions where he could leverage his sales, customer relations, and communications skills.

If you, like Pete Bianchi, suffer from less than top-notch strategic thinking ability, I suggest you employ some of the same techniques that Pete did:

- Evaluate your team, and look for opportunities to add staff with strong strategic skills and a willingness to challenge conventional wisdom about how things are done.

- Avoid the tendency to think you have to be the source of all strategic wisdom for your group. Involve others in strategic discussions and brainstorming events. Like Pete, consider playing a facilitator role focused on leading the discussion of strategic issues and opportunities—as opposed to feeling that you have to generate new strategies all by yourself.

- Use your communication skills to motivate others to embrace the new strategy you and your team have developed.

Clearly it's preferable to have outstanding strategic gears as a leader. However, you'll get the credit if your company's senior executives see breakthrough strategies emerging from your team and if you are successful in inspiring others to mobilize behind a new sense of strategic direction.

DEMONSTRATING STRATEGIC THINKING ABILITY IN A STAFF OR FUNCTIONAL ROLE

Managers in staff functions such as finance or human resources are often perplexed about how to display their strategic skills given the support nature of their organizations. In reality, the bar for strategic thinking is set higher for business unit leaders than it is for heads of support functions. Business unit heads and leaders of customer-facing groups such as marketing and sales must pursue a number of important activities in developing strategy: tracking underlying marketplace trends, such as changes in consumer demographics or the introduction of new technologies; finding ways to understand and anticipate customer needs; analyzing the strategies of competitors; and, ultimately, generating the strategic insight that serves as the basis for a successful new business strategy.

By contrast, leaders of staff support functions are required to anticipate how to direct their groups to support the company's overall strategy. Based on a deep understanding of the business's strategy, they need to take the initiative in building the programs, systems, and staff capability needed to implement the overall company strategy. In addition, they need to identify the major industry trends in their functional areas that are likely to have an impact on the company. For an HR department, it can be anticipating changes in the supply, demand, and cost of employing staff; for government affairs, it might be preparing for potential new governmental regulations; and for a corporate finance department, assessing the impact of new financial practices may be a priority.

In their strategic planning, many functional groups spend time defining the department's value proposition (the unique set of services the department will provide to the company) and creating plans designed to deliver on that value proposition. As was the case with Phil Whalen's HR strategic planning initiative, defining a value proposition for a functional department typically starts with identifying the group's most important customers (both internal and external to the organization), highlighting the major needs of those customers, and determining how the department can best meet those needs.

One information technology (IT) department I worked with spent a considerable amount of time talking to internal customers and tracking developments in the IT marketplace. Based on this work, they revised their department strategy and reorganized the department to align with that strategy. Their new value proposition was based on serving as partners who could help internal groups find ways to apply technology to serve the company's external consumers while streamlining operations. As a result of this new strategy, roundly endorsed by the corporation's senior executives, the IT management team increased the proportion of staff who worked directly with internal customer groups and reduced the number of staff involved in creating new IT programs. Their new strategy assumed that they could buy more of the IT programs they needed from external vendors and that the department's greatest value stemmed from close interaction with internal customers across the company.

Although the focus of strategic planning for a functional group varies from that of a business unit, once the strategy for a staff support group is developed, the manager's task becomes the same as that of any other business leader:

- Translating the new strategy into a tangible set of priorities to guide the work of department staff

- Selling the new strategy and priorities to senior management

- Communicating the new strategy to internal groups across the company and to departmental staff in a clear, compelling way

If you aspire to lead a functional organization at the C-suite level, don't lose sight of the fact that strategic thinking applies to these roles just as it does to business unit leadership jobs. Those who make executive promotion decisions will still look for your ability to think long term and anticipate the kind of support the business needs from your functional area.

AVOIDING THE FIRST LIEUTENANT SYNDROME

Although all managers aren't created equal in terms of their strategic abilities, on occasion I've seen otherwise talented managers fall victim to what I call the first lieutenant syndrome. It's a pitfall to avoid. Recall that in Chapter One, Mike Peterson, an otherwise highly successful manager, was being held back in large part by concerns about his strategic thinking skills. In Mike's case, part of the problem was that his abilities were overshadowed by the highly strategic and visionary boss he had reported to for several years. Such a situation creates a real dilemma since the fruits of the manager's strategic thinking may go unnoticed as the organization attributes the manager's contributions to his boss.

If you find yourself in a situation like this, you'll have to initiate a patient yet persistent conversation with your boss to avoid being pegged as a strong number two for the rest of your career. You may need to enlist your manager's help to engineer a move to a new assignment in another part of the organization where you can demonstrate your strategic abilities independent of your boss. Alternatively, you and your manager may be able to identify a major initiative with significant strategic content that you can lead in your current position. In that case, your boss can support you by helping showcase the results of the initiative to senior management so you get credit for your work and, in the process, build a reputation for strategic thinking in your own right.

FOCUSING ON THE CONTROLLABLE FACTORS

This chapter began with an observation that's not at all surprising: creating a winning strategy and imparting a sense of direction to the organization are the most fundamental tasks of any executive. Some portion of strategic thinking ability is innate. You can't change that hardwiring, but you can maximize your natural strategic ability. Rather than lose sleep over your innate abilities, I suggest you focus on the elements of strategic thinking that you can control: educating yourself about strategy, taking steps to feed your strategic intelligence, broadening your perspective on the business and the industry, and developing your ability to communicate a strategic vision in a compelling way. Clearly all of this takes time. To free up the time and share of mind required for strategic thinking, you'll need to rely on your team: a team you can delegate to, a team you can trust to ensure that new strategies and priorities are implemented as planned. And that leads to the second critical factor of executive selection: your ability to build a strong management team.

CHAPTER 4

FACTOR 2
Building a Strong Management Team

S mart managers quickly figure out that their success depends on the capability of their team. Virtually all of the factors that are critical to executive advancement require that leaders can rely on their staff to perform. Interacting with customers and other external groups, carving out time for strategic thinking, identifying the next big breakthrough, influencing and persuading peers across the company: all of these take time, and a strong team allows you to focus on them.

Much has been written about people management recently and how great leaders engage their teams and develop their people. These books emphasize team communications, providing performance feedback, coaching, training, conducting team-building sessions, building team morale, and so forth. Certainly all of these are good things, and I truly wish that every manager was skilled in doing them. However, when I participate in succession planning discussions, I'm interested in what's critical to senior executives when they talk about a manager's "people management skills"—and what's less important when they make promotion decisions. I've seen managers with mediocre people skills get promoted while others who truly care about their people end up sitting on the sidelines. What makes the difference?

There's an old expression, to "major in the majors," meaning to pay attention to the most important priorities. The managers I see who get promoted to the executive level may not necessarily be kinder and gentler than other managers. They may fall short on certain aspects of people management. Their people might prefer more direct feedback and more frequent team-building sessions to foster their sense of being a team. But these managers focus on the one key lever that is critical to building a strong management team: surrounding themselves with talented staff members who collectively form a strong team.

For executives who make decisions about promotions to the C-suite level, talent is king. They look for managers with the proverbial nose for talent and the determination required to build a strong team of highly skilled staff. Specifically, in evaluating candidates for executive-level positions, they look for evidence of the following. Can this individual

- Identify the range of skills required within the team?
- Attract people with that kind of talent?

- Objectively evaluate the strengths and weaknesses of staff members and determine the assignments to allow people to perform and develop?

- Create an adequate level of clarity within the team about roles and responsibilities and an adequate level of team cohesion and morale?

And, finally, senior-level decision makers look for a manager's track record of having developed talent on behalf of the company.

To illustrate different approaches to building a management team, consider the stories of Anita Richardson and Craig Gallagher, two managers I worked closely with. Although Anita wasn't the warm and fuzzy type, she was able to assemble a talented management team. Over the years, Craig had fallen into some bad habits, but when faced with a need to strengthen his team, he rose to the challenge.

Anita Richardson

Anita Richardson was described by those who worked with her as pleasant and invariably composed but a bit reserved. A highly talented and hard-driving manager, she made it clear that her ultimate career goal was to become chief financial officer of the company, a global financial services firm. Although always professional in her approach, Anita projected an attitude that nothing was ever good

71

enough. On a regular basis in her team meetings, she could be expected to repeat her mantra: that everyone in the group, including herself, needed to improve his skills by 10 percent each year.

Anita had taken over as head of finance for one of the company's major business units two years ago. Within the first few months, she made two staff changes and brought in two people from outside the company. At first, these steps were somewhat controversial given the corporation's reputation for encouraging long job tenure and loyalty to the company. However, within a few months, there was widespread agreement that both new people were excellent and that the overall quality of Anita's staff had improved substantially.

Anita had a reputation for being a bit distant from her people and admitted that she hated doing annual performance reviews with her staff. However, when her boss attended her annual people review sessions, he marveled at the thoroughness of her presentations. She had a clear understanding of each direct report's strengths, limitations, motivational drivers, and career goals. Although she had never disclosed this publicly, she confided to her human resource manager that she had a long-term plan to upgrade her team's talent level through promoting, developing, reassigning, and recruiting staff members.

Anita felt comfortable hiring strong people who were willing to challenge the status quo and push back on her, even in public settings. She devoted considerable time to networking within the company and was always on the lookout for talent she might bring into her group. Once staff members had earned her confidence, she provided them with considerable leeway in managing their areas. Her top performers found themselves pushed and challenged to take on responsibility for new tasks. Although not a hand holder of staff, she provided her people with direct feedback at the end of major projects and helped them learn from their experiences.

Some members of the team complained that roles and responsibilities within the department were not entirely clear and that occasionally people might bump into one another when working on departmental initiatives. Anita spent time with her team making sure that responsibilities within the team were clear on major projects. However, she expressed concern about creating a sense of bureaucracy within her group. She felt that defining people's roles too precisely could become an organizational straitjacket and a barrier to the sense of initiative she wanted staff members to display. As a result, she was prepared to accept the friction among her people that sometimes cropped up.

Over time a number of her best people were tapped for promotion to other positions within the company, something noted by the corporation's chief financial officer (CFO) and other senior executives. As a result of her strong financial skills and ability to create a strong team, the CFO began a series of discussions with Anita about new assignments that would round out her skills with an eye to her becoming CFO in the future.

Craig Gallagher

Craig Gallagher was a born salesman and a long-time fixture within his industry. For a number of years, he had led an important business unit for his company, a large natural resources corporation. The kind of personable and enthusiastic leader that everybody loved, he had parlayed his sales and customer relationship skills into an enviable record of growth for his division. Based on favorable trends within the industry, a recent corporate strategic planning review had targeted Craig's business for considerable investment to continue its growth. This decision focused attention on the strength of Craig's organization.

As this strategic plan was being initiated, Craig was selected to participate in a leadership assessment and development program sponsored by the corporation. As part of Craig's assessment, I interviewed his boss and a number of his peers and direct reports. Both Craig and the corporation's CEO awaited the results eagerly, given the company's plan to invest in Craig's business.

The assessment produced some conflicting results. There was no question that Craig was well respected within the company's management group. He was also a bit of a father figure within his division. Highly trusted personally, his industry knowledge was second to none, and his network within the industry had helped put the company on the map with customers and industry groups. However, the assessment highlighted some troubling issues that were magnified now that Craig's division was poised for rapid growth.

The feedback from the assessment suggested that Craig was a really nice guy—too nice a guy, in fact. Over the years, he had recruited several people he had come to know in the course of his career and was seen as overly loyal to them. Although Craig's peers respected him personally and viewed him as highly collaborative, they felt he had surrounded himself with a weak team. Both his direct reports and his peers felt that on occasion he had accepted mediocre performance and shied away from having tough conversations with his people. In certain situations, he had worked around deficiencies on the part of his staff by changing their roles as opposed to dealing with the problem directly.

My feedback session with Craig was a difficult one. He was polite and professional as we went through the results of his assessment. It was clear, though, that his peers' belief that he had a weak team hit him hard. As I often do, I followed up with Craig a few days later. He told me that he had experienced a "dark night of the soul" (a weekend actually) as he thought through the feedback I had provided. At one point, he even thought about resigning from the company. Instead he decided to attack the problem head-on. He enlisted members of a corporate staff group to help him think through the organization structure and level of expertise he would need to develop the business as planned. The staff members also worked with him to objectively evaluate his existing team members against the requirements of the positions within the new structure.

At that point, Craig went to work, and within two months, he had reorganized his entire team. His best performers remained, but one of his direct reports left the organization, and another accepted a lesser role. He also began recruiting outside the company for two positions on his team. As he put his new team in place, he conducted conversations with each direct report to convey the level of performance he wanted and how he expected his new team to operate.

Normally a change like this creates consternation within an organization. In this case, however, Craig's new staff described a sense of fresh air flowing through the business unit.

STEPS TO BUILD A STRONG MANAGEMENT TEAM

Building a strong management team requires painstaking work. However, successful executives recognize that surrounding themselves with a talented team allows them to leverage their contribution within the organization. To build the management strength that allows them to do so, they focus their efforts in five areas:

- Creating and implementing a plan to continuously upgrade talent within their team
- Proactively attracting talent
- Motivating and developing people through challenging assignments
- Stepping up to performance issues
- Creating an adequate level of role clarity and cohesion within the team

Some managers make the mistake of trying to develop the people they inherit when taking on a new position. By contrast, those with a track record for developing strong management teams start with a clear understanding of the talent level required and then work persistently to achieve it.

Planning to Upgrade Talent Within the Team

Executives who are successful in building a strong management team start by considering two fundamental questions:

1. What set of skills and expertise do I need on the team to accomplish the organization's goals and allow my organization to succeed?

2. As a leader, where should I be spending my time, and how can I add the greatest value to the company?

In a very real sense such executives view their team and their organization as an extension of themselves. As a result, they give a lot of thought to where on the team they need to upgrade talent and where they need to put in place people with skills that complement their own.

Based on the answers to these questions, they identify the steps necessary to build their team. For example, they may bring onto the team people to whom they can delegate responsibility for certain areas so they can focus their own efforts on a more limited number of high-priority areas; people with specific expertise, like in-depth financial analysis or customer relationship building, that complement their own skills; strong strategic thinkers to bolster their own capabilities; "go-to" people who have strong administrative skills and can stay on top of implementation activities; or creative thinkers who will challenge them and their team to think in new ways and see new opportunities.

Building a strong team requires planning and persistence—and often a large dose of patience. It typically takes months and years to achieve the team strength that will allow you to drive the business and play the value-added role you have envisioned for yourself. Managers who are successful in building strong management teams are similar in some respects to coaches of professional sports teams: they want their teams to win this year—in the case of business executives, to accomplish their annual performance goals. But they also want the team to be stronger next year—and the year after that. As a result, they are always tweaking the roster and bringing in better players so the team continues to get stronger.

In building their team strength, many executives consider the team's mix of A, B, and C players:

A players: Those who not only are top performers today but can grow in the course of their careers.

B players: Those who are steady, proficient performers in their current jobs or at their current level. B players often possess specialized skills or experience important to the organization's success.

C players: Those who are either not performing today (perhaps because they're in the wrong job) or whose skills are falling behind the curve as the business grows more demanding and complex. In top-performing companies, C players are quickly moved to new assignments that fit better with their skills—or new jobs outside the company.

Having a team composed of all A players is every manager's dream—but it's a luxury few companies can afford. As a manager, your focus should be on increasing the proportion of A players on your team while helping the B players increase their skills and contribution. Realize that A players are motivated by the same desire for career advancement that you are. Since the contribution of top performers is so important to their ability to achieve their business objectives, some managers try to block them from taking on new assignments and attempt to slow their career progress. Savvy managers understand that A players want to move ahead in the organization. As a result, they play an active role in career planning with them. Although it's always difficult when one of your top people leaves your team, you'll reap the benefits in the long term. When others in the organization see your success in developing and promoting talented people, attracting rising stars to your team becomes much easier for you.

One of the pluses of having a plan to upgrade the strength of your team is that it allows you to anticipate—as opposed to react to—staff changes. Again, it may take months and years to fully implement your plan, but the team will be getting stronger along the way. And if you are successful, you're likely to have moved up to a higher-level position, where the cycle of building your team begins again.

Taking the Initiative to Attract Talent

Some managers focus on developing the staff they inherited and view recruiting as a way to fill openings when they occur. By contrast, executives who are successful in building their management teams start by determining the strength they need. And then they view every staff opening as an opportunity to move toward their talent goal. Furthermore, they recognize that adding fresh blood to the team can have a secondary benefit: raising the performance bar within the team. Often the addition of one or two new A players with great skills and a strong drive to excel has the effect of motivating existing team members to up their game.

Managers like Anita Richardson don't simply wait for a position on their teams to open up. They actively troll for talent within the company and are prepared to recruit externally when necessary. Importantly, in filling a position they don't just focus on finding someone who can do the job. They also look for growth potential—the ability to expand in the job and take on positions of more responsibility in the future.

So keep your eye out for rising stars across the company who may be candidates to join your team at some point in the future. Look for opportunities to get to know them better and build a relationship. For example, offer to serve as a mentor. Find ways, such as attending conferences or joining an industry or professional group, to meet people outside the company. At a minimum, meeting a broad range of people allows you to calibrate or compare the skills of your team members with the external marketplace. You may find someone who would be a great addition to your team when the time is right.

Motivating and Developing People Through Challenging Assignments

I'm always interested in how managers go about developing their people. For some managers, their first instinct is to send people to training programs to develop their skills. However, if training is the main arrow in their developmental quiver, they are often disappointed by the results. By contrast, managers who are most successful in developing their people turn first to challenging assignments—and reinforce such on-the-job learning with training and coaching as appropriate.

The kinds of assignments that will prove challenging and developmental vary considerably by individual. So spend time with your direct reports to understand their strengths, weaknesses, and experience gaps, as well as their goals and interests. Where are they trying to go in their careers, and what kind of experiences would quicken their pulse? For an upwardly mobile A player, it's likely to be an assignment that will increase his visibility within the organization and build new skills. For a highly valued B player, it may be getting to know a new part of the business or access to state-of-the-art advances in her area of expertise.

Devoting time to career planning discussions with direct reports tends to generate loyalty on their part. They'll appreciate your efforts to help them define their career goals and find ways to achieve them. Knowing where your people want to go helps you in two

82

ways: identifying the assignments in their current jobs that will motivate them and contribute to their growth, and helping you move them on to new jobs within the company at the right time—thus creating an opportunity to implement your plan to upgrade talent within the team.

Stepping Up to Performance Issues

Craig Gallagher's story illustrates all too well the problems of procrastination in dealing with performance problems within your team. Whether it's a subpar performer or a person who's in the wrong job, allowing a performance problem to fester has several negative consequences. Such situations lower performance standards within your team and sap energy from your organization. Working around performance issues, as Craig Gallagher attempted to do, leads to confusion and inefficiency within your team. Having to work alongside subpar performers also tends to turn off your A players since they'll sense a double standard. At the extreme, I've seen managers, sometimes motivated by the best of intentions, cover for underperformers on their teams. Whenever you stoop to do your direct reports' work or make decisions for them, you're diverting yourself from activities where you can add the most value—and thus you are weakening your team's overall performance.

Stepping up to such situations doesn't suggest you have to be brutal or precipitous. Rather, it involves a willingness on your part to have what can be difficult conversations.

But remember: it's important to let people know where they stand and where they need to improve. Some people will be able to respond to your feedback. With others, you'll have to help them find a new home in a new role that's a better fit with their skills—whether inside or outside the company. Without a doubt, this is one of the hardest parts of managing people. However, if you avoid it, all of your other efforts to build a strong team will go for naught.

Creating an Adequate Level of Role Clarity and Team Cohesion

So far, I've emphasized the importance of attracting and developing talent to build a strong management team. That's the crucial priority—but I don't want to leave you with the impression that building a sense of team among your direct reports is unimportant. Successful executives devote time to team building—they just don't make it their primary focus in building the strength of their team.

Such executives strive for enough clarity regarding roles so that people can do their jobs and team members know how and when to support each other. As an example, shortly after taking over as head of a new management group, one executive I know took the team off-site so he could explain how he wanted team members to work together. Over the course of two days, the group completed some typical team-building exercises: sharing

84

information about their styles as individuals and defining desired behaviors such as openness, trust, and collaboration. At that point the team got pretty tactical. They explored what the new leader called "points of intersection and leverage": areas where the work of team members connected and where collaboration was most important. They also identified the major decisions the group needed to make and defined how the team would interact with the leader in making those decisions. According to the leader, his direct reports had areas of job responsibility that were relatively distinct from one another. Rather than mandate a team approach where it didn't add value, he wanted the team to be clear about their accountabilities and how they would work together when it truly contributed to the team's success. Once he had taken these steps to "chalk the field," to create a general sense of roles within the team, he felt the team could go back to work—and he could continue to focus on upgrading the talent within the team over time.

BUILDING A STRONG MANAGEMENT TEAM: THE IMPACT OF ORGANIZATIONAL CULTURE

At this point, you may be asking yourself: "All these suggestions about building a strong management team may be fine, but how could I do that in my company? The system won't let me!" In reality, companies' staffing and talent development practices vary widely, and organizational cultures play a big role in how managers can deploy these techniques. Companies' practices differ in a number of ways:

- Their approach to dealing with performance issues and the value the company places on tenure within the company
- The relative emphasis placed on hiring from outside versus filling positions internally
- How long people are typically expected to stay in a position before moving to a new job
- The relative ease of people moving to new assignments across group or department lines
- Management's willingness to stretch compensation guidelines to hire highly talented people from outside the company

Since such practices and the cultural norms surrounding staffing and people management vary significantly, it's incumbent on you to understand your company's practices—as well as how far and how fast you can push the envelope to put in place the strong management team you need. In some companies, significant changes to your team can be accomplished in six to twelve months. In other companies—with different practices—it may take two or even three years. Regardless of your company's culture, the important thing is to have a plan: the positions you need to upgrade, the people you can stretch to take on new responsibilities, and the openings you'll use to bring in people with new skills and growth potential. The speed at which you can implement your plan may have to be adjusted to your company's practices. But don't lose sight of your ultimate goal: to surround yourself with a team of strong players who will enable you to achieve your goals and those of the organization.

BUILDING YOUR MANAGEMENT TEAM: A MATTER OF FOCUS

Before concluding this chapter I want to be clear about one thing: I am not casting aspersions on managers who are conscientious about providing their staff members with performance feedback and coaching and skilled at creating a high level of team morale. I think these things are great and will add to your success as a manager. Moreover, training—for the right person at the right time with the right reinforcement—can be tremendously valuable. Just keep in mind the definition of "building a strong management team" that senior-level decision makers have when they consider people for C-suite positions. That's the ability to surround yourself with talented people who collectively create a strong team and can produce results consistently.

As you look for ways to demonstrate your ability to build a strong management team, let me challenge you with one final question: Do your direct reports' skills allow you to focus on the business's most critical issues and play the value-added role you've envisioned for yourself? If the answer to that question is "no" or "not quite," that's very telling. Your next step is to use the tools I've outlined to create and implement a plan to upgrade your team.

CHAPTER 5

FACTOR 3
Managing Implementation

Strategic thinking and the ability to impart a vision are critical elements of an executive's skill set. However, never lose sight of the fact that the ability to go from strategy to implementation—to "operationalize the insight," as Ron Williams, the CEO of Aetna, says—remains a fundamental task for any executive. Your responsibility to execute your strategic priorities in a predictable way doesn't change as you move up the organization. What does change is how you manage the transition from strategy to execution. At lower levels in the company, you are likely to be centrally involved in seeing that work gets done in a high-quality and predictable manner. As you progress toward the executive ranks, though, your emphasis needs to change. That shift entails building and reinforcing what I call an infrastructure that promotes implementation without your having to be involved in every detail. In essence, your challenge is to ensure that the wash gets out the door—without having to divert your time and energy away from the other roles you must play at the executive level: dealing with customers, crafting strategy, building your team, and so forth.

Those who make decisions about promotions to the C-suite level start by looking at a person's track record for producing consistent results, one of the nonnegotiable factors described in Chapter One. Then they look for answers to the following questions. Can this individual

- Focus the attention of the organization on the timely implementation of strategic priorities and initiatives?

- Take large goals and break them down into discrete action steps with clearly defined accountabilities?

- Put in place the roles, processes, and follow-up mechanisms that ensure timely execution?

- Ensure the predictable implementation of major priorities and initiatives without undue personal involvement at too low a level of detail?

Most successful managers first make their mark as doers who know how to get things done by being centrally involved in working with others. To progress to the executive level, you'll need to demonstrate your ability to build your team's capacity for implementation and rely on others to handle many—but not all—of the details on your behalf. To illustrate this core selection factor, consider the stories of two very different managers.

Lee Monroe

Any executive coach would like to tell you that he's been 100 percent successful in his coaching assignments. I wish it were true, but it's not. Like any other coach, I've worked with managers I couldn't get through to or who were too ingrained in their habits to change. Lee Monroe was one of them.

Lee was used to being the smartest person in the room in virtually every situation he encountered. He worked for a large medical supply corporation and two years ago had been promoted to general manager of the company's most important business unit. Five years before that, he had been recruited from a small start-up firm. In his first position with the company, where he led a small, fast-growing business, Lee had produced impressive results. His new, much larger unit had historically been very profitable but now faced intense competition. This more aggressive competition combined with recently announced industry regulations to reduce the unit's profit margins. Lee's new role was a big jump in responsibility, and he and his team were charged with increasing the unit's profitability and restoring its rate of growth. Given the unit's importance to the company, Lee's performance was highly visible to the corporation's senior management.

Before beginning my work with Lee, I met with his manager. She told me that the members of the company's senior leadership team were highly invested in seeing Lee succeed. However, she had received some troubling feedback from several of Lee's team members. Although Lee was still viewed as an immense talent, there was widespread concern that he was spreading himself too thin: he was involved in too many issues and wasn't delegating enough. She had shared this feedback with Lee but wasn't sure she'd gotten through to him.

Armed with this background, I met with Lee, and we agreed that I would conduct a series of confidential interviews with members of his team as well as peers in other units across the company. What came out of the interviews was extremely consistent—and sobering. Everyone I interviewed agreed that Lee was a high-integrity manager with great intentions and that he combined a fierce intellect with terrific industry experience. His peers saw him as highly collaborative and committed to the company's best interests. However, the level of frustration expressed by his direct reports and others within his division was profound.

Simply put, Lee was a micromanager who wasn't able to trust his people fully. He claimed that his approach was to delegate all but the most important decisions to his direct reports. However, his team members countered that Lee needed to approve virtually all of their decisions and was prone to second-guessing their work. Although Lee professed a desire to empower his team, his calendar was filled with meetings on a wide range of projects and initiatives. His direct reports complained that they were hauled into interminable meetings to discuss issues, but it was clear that Lee would make the ultimate decision. He was widely described as a perfectionist who wanted to be 100 percent sure before making a decision or approving a project. Over the past year, progress within the division had slowed to a halt. Often Lee and his calendar were the bottleneck to progress. He always seemed to be able to spot a way to improve a project plan. The consequent re-do's, however, led to new action items and even more meetings.

Lee liked to describe himself as a "player-coach" who could contribute to and guide the team's efforts. Although that may have been his intention, his direct reports complained that they were never sure which of Lee's comments was a brainstorm and which were directives. They said that follow-up actions and responsibilities were often left unclear when a meeting ended—with Lee rushing out the door to get to his next meeting.

This situation had been brewing for some time before I got involved, and it seemed to be getting worse as the pressure on the division for improved performance grew. Lee responded professionally to the feedback I gave him, acknowledging that it was consistent with the feedback he'd received from his boss. As we talked, he told me that he'd never failed in anything in his life and was "hell-bent and determined" to see the unit succeed under his leadership. I encouraged him to think seriously about where he wanted to focus his time and energy and find more opportunities to delegate decisions and tasks to members of his team. As we talked, he confided in me that although he liked each of his staff members personally, he wasn't fully comfortable delegating major decisions to any of them. His plan was to coach them, hoping that from their interaction with him, they'd get to the point when they were capable of going it alone. In response, I warned him of the dangers of being intimately involved in so many issues and relayed the sense of gridlock I had picked up in the interviews.

Over the next six months, Lee never demonstrated any real change, and that led to a growing sense of frustration within the division. It didn't come as a total surprise when his key number two person, a manager with strong operational skills, announced her resignation to join another company. Two other members of the team left as well.

Lee was never able to let go, trust his people, and build the capability of his organization to function without his direct involvement. Due to his intelligence, experience, and sheer hard work, he was able to keep his division afloat for two more years. However, the unit never returned to its previous levels of profitability. Although once highly regarded by the company, Lee's career stalled, and he ended up leaving to pursue other opportunities.

Vivien Campbell

I met Viv Campbell when we worked together in a leadership assessment and development program that her company, a global publishing giant, made available to high-potential managers like her. Given my ongoing relationship with Viv's company, I was able to track her progress even after we stopped working together directly. After my first meeting with her, I was impressed by the level of clarity she showed about the kind of organization she wanted to build and her knowledge of the different levers that would help her achieve her goals. What was even more impressive was her ability to shift gears and modify her approach as her efforts began to take hold.

When I began working with Viv, she had started to settle in as general manager of a business unit that was often referred to as the problem child of the corporation. Although the team that she inherited had a number of experienced and willing managers, the unit's growth rate had not been impressive; in fact, it had failed to meet its targets for several years in a row. Highly competitive, Viv set out to improve the unit's performance and build the unit's capacity to execute its plans.

Viv was a great believer in planning that was intensive, detailed, action oriented, and team based. After taking over as GM, she scheduled a number of planning meetings with her direct reports once her unit's performance targets had been established by the corporation. More tactical than strategic, these meetings produced a set of priorities that she and her team members all signed up for. Each priority was broken down into a number of specific action steps with timetables and accountabilities assigned to each action. In a number of instances, multiple departments within the unit needed to work together on a priority, and these areas were clearly highlighted. At the conclusion of these planning meetings, the priorities were made part of each team member's annual performance goals.

Viv worked with her team members to institutionalize these priorities and keep them front and center in the minds of everyone in the unit. Whenever possible, quantitative metrics were established for each priority, and updates on the status of each metric were shared at Viv's monthly staff meetings. Progress against the metrics was also highlighted in monthly memos sent out to the unit's employees and in the quarterly all-hands meetings that Viv and her team held with employees. In those meetings and in virtually all communications to unit staff, Viv and her direct reports made a point of recognizing individual contribution to implementing the unit's priorities.

During her first year as GM, Viv scheduled regular meetings to review the status of the team's priorities. As team members updated the group, she didn't hesitate to get involved in a considerable level of detail. Patiently yet persistently, she tested staff members' depth of thinking about issues. She also probed to ensure that accountabilities and implementation timetables had been clearly established and were being met. Through her questions, Viv made it abundantly clear that she expected each team member to have an intimate knowledge of his area and the status of its action items.

The unit's performance improved that first year, but it didn't quite reach the level of achievement Viv and her team had set. As she began her second year as GM, Viv took stock of her unit's progress toward instituting a culture of implementation. While not reducing her emphasis on execution, she looked for ways to build on the team's momentum and change how she was spending her time, since so much of the implementation effort revolved around her. After reflection, she alerted her team to expect some changes in her approach.

She and the team conducted the same set of planning meetings they had the prior year. They updated the unit's performance metrics to reflect the new set of priorities established, and they recommitted to communicating updates on the priorities to all unit employees throughout the course of the year. Then Viv announced to her team that she had asked the manager of the operations area, one of her direct reports, to play an informal chief of staff role within the team. Highly organized personally, the operations manager became the keeper of the team's action and follow-up log—a role that Viv had previously performed.

It was in her staff meetings and individual meetings with direct reports that her team began to see a major change in Viv's approach. On most issues, she pressed team members for less information about projects than in the past. However, she made it clear that she expected them to stay on top of the details of their respective areas and alert her to any initiatives that were heading off track. By contrast, she began to focus most of her questions on a more limited set of topics, to the point that her direct reports began to anticipate her questions and include answers in their periodic update meetings. By focusing her questions on a few key topics (for example, the impact of major initiatives on customers and other parts of the corporate organization, potential reaction by competitors, and the support needed to ensure execution), she found that she was successful in getting her people to be proactive in considering the right issues.

When a couple of major initiatives began to fall behind schedule, her team realized that Viv was still prepared to roll up her sleeves and jump in if there was a problem to fix. These deep dives, however, were the exception, as Viv consciously increased her level of delegation to those direct reports who had demonstrated the ability to stay on top of their responsibilities. As she began to delegate more, she outlined to her direct reports where their decision-making authority lay. She was also clear about the areas where they could expect her to continue to be centrally involved.

In her second year as GM, Viv scheduled fewer team update meetings as she increasingly relied on the operations manager and one-on-one meetings with direct reports to track the progress of major initiatives. Although she held fewer team meetings to review the status of priorities, update sessions were still thorough and guidelines for preparation well defined. In the course of these meetings, staff members saw her slowly pull back in terms of the number of decisions she weighed in on.

Viv's efforts were highly successful in raising her unit's performance and increasing her team's reputation as a group that could predictably achieve its goals. Not surprisingly, her career star continued to rise within the company. She had shown her ability to move into a difficult assignment and build the organization's capacity to execute. As a result, her manager was instrumental in arranging a new job for her in the corporate strategic planning department. This job was designed to build on her proven implementation skills and position her for larger executive positions in the future.

BUILDING AN INFRASTRUCTURE OF IMPLEMENTATION

To be in the running for promotion to the C-suite level, you'll have demonstrated one of the nonnegotiable factors highlighted in Chapter One: a track record for producing consistently strong results. You'll also have displayed the ability to get things done—but often within the context of a small team where you can get your arms around all of the implementation details. To build others' confidence in your ability to lead execution at the executive level, you will need to convince those who make executive selection decisions that you can scale your own efforts and manage implementation within a larger organization. As you do so, you'll also need to project a sense that you have the capacity to take on more responsibility given your success in leveraging your own efforts through others.

99

To some extent, your ability to manage implementation, without being inordinately involved in the details, is a function of the strength of the team you've inherited and its capacity for execution. However, you can learn a lot from Viv Campbell and the two phases she pursued to create a culture of implementation within her team: building the foundation and then elevating your game.

BUILDING THE FOUNDATION

Strengthening your team's capacity for implementation typically requires some basic blocking and tackling—and considerable persistence on your part. The executives I've seen who are successful in building this type of foundation focus on three elements of implementation: intensive action planning, establishing follow-up mechanisms, and putting in place reinforcers designed to focus the attention of the organization on implementation.

Action Planning and Follow-Up Mechanisms

Your first step in building the foundation for implementation is straightforward but rarely easy: taking your strategic goals and priorities and working with your team to break them down into specific action steps and accountabilities. These are the eyehooks of execution you and your team can latch onto. I've seen very senior executives devote considerable time to team planning meetings in the attempt to focus their organization on execution. In addition to specifying accountabilities, they work with their teams to identify areas where direct reports and their teams need to communicate and collaborate closely. They pay special attention to handoffs between groups—where responsibility shifts from one person or team to another—since these are the areas where things are most likely to fall through the cracks.

They also work with their teams to put in place follow-up mechanisms to ensure that everything is on track. Some are as simple as monthly reports or planned updates during regularly scheduled staff meetings. Depending on the complexity of the initiative and the team's capacity for implementation, some leaders go further and schedule quarterly team off-site meetings to review implementation progress. Such leaders recognize that good intentions aren't enough to ensure execution. A regular cadence of follow-up activities helps people to focus on the implementation of priorities. And bringing the team of direct reports together generates a positive peer pressure since no team member wants to be the one who let the organization down.

Focusing the Organization's Attention

In most companies, many things conspire to divert a team's emphasis away from implementing its plans. People tell me that multiple and shifting priorities or excitement over a new opportunity can take the organization's eye off the ball. To counteract this, make sure you put in place ways to reinforce implementation. Many teams create metrics to measure their success in implementing their priorities. Often these metrics are put on scorecards that are displayed throughout the organization and, as was the case with Viv Campbell, embedded in the performance objectives of each direct report. In some companies, I've seen this take the form of dashboards that display the scorecard on the computer screen of each team member when she turns on her computer each morning.

Consider also your communication to your organization to make sure it reinforces the type of implementation you want. Whether it's in written memos to staff or all-employee meetings, spotlight the organization's success in executing its plans and priorities. In your communication, recognize individuals and teams that are exhibiting the performance-related behavior you want. For example, highlight people who are collaborating in the interest of implementing key priorities or going to great lengths to surmount obstacles to execution. In this way, you're signaling the kind of behavior you want to promote within the organization.

In building your organization's capacity for implementation, don't neglect one other important reinforcer: compensation and reward. In many companies, goal setting and compensation are a pretty hit-or-miss affair, where people's compensation is not well aligned with implementation requirements. Few performance management systems are perfect, but I suggest you try to maximize the impact of the one your company has. It's important for people to know that their success in implementing major priorities will be rewarded. Over time as a manager, you get what you pay for. So be prepared to make distinctions among your direct reports in their performance ratings, salary, and bonus based on their contribution to implementing agreed-on priorities.

At times this can lead to some difficult but important conversations with your staff. I once worked with a manager who was committed to improving performance in the business unit he had recently taken over, and improving the unit's level of execution was a key to achieving that performance. During his first year, his team really came together around the priorities they established together. However, some team members fell short in achieving their objectives in certain areas. When performance review time came, team members learned that this manager encouraged effort but rewarded results. Over the next year, both individual and group performance continued to improve.

ELEVATING YOUR GAME

Building your team's foundation for implementation is vitally important, and you never want to deemphasize execution. However, if you are successful in training your team to execute, your next priority is to reduce your involvement at the detailed level while still building your organization's capacity to implement. Use these levers to do so:

- Institute follow-up roles.
- Delegate and clarify roles in decision making.
- Use the power of repetitive questions.
- Identify and eliminate obstacles to execution.

Instituting Follow-Up Roles

To begin to distance yourself from detailed involvement in most or all of your team's priorities, consider designating a highly organized staff member to take on some of the follow-up activity on your behalf. Whether it's a chief of staff, such as Viv Campbell employed, or a member of your team designated to monitor the accomplishment of agreed-on tasks, having someone play this role can reduce the time you spend in day-to-day follow-up. He'll also be your early-warning system if implementation plans are in danger of getting off track.

Leveraging Yourself Through Delegation

As the scope of your responsibilities grows, you'll need to sharpen your ability to delegate to your staff—while still making sure that major initiatives proceed as planned. Some managers, like Lee Monroe, never feel comfortable delegating to their team, but not learning to rely on your team limits your success, as it did with Lee.

As your team gains experience in managing implementation, think carefully about where you want to focus your time and attention. What are the key issues or initiatives where you want to be centrally involved? Usually your choice is based on the importance of the priority or the experience you can bring to bear. By contrast, where can you delegate tasks, decisions, or areas of responsibility to team members? As an example of delegating an area of responsibility, one manager of new product development I know has a direct report whom he relies on to manage field tests of new product concepts. The manager devotes a great deal of time to working with others on breakthrough ideas for new products. He reviews the results of field-test activity with his direct report but doesn't get involved otherwise unless there's a problem.

As you attempt to delegate more, also think through your involvement in decision making. If you need to make or approve virtually every decision in your area, you're not really delegating much authority. In fact, you become a bottleneck for your organization and diminish its capacity for implementation. Be careful in choosing the decisions you need to make or approve, because the more you touch a decision, the more you'll need to master the details of the situation.

Using the Power of Repetitive Questions

As their teams become more skilled in implementation, I see a number of successful executives begin to employ a subtle but highly effective questioning technique, one I encourage you to adopt. In their book *Execution: The Discipline of Getting Things Done*, Larry Bossidy and Ram Charan describe the questions Bossidy employed to focus people's attention in the course of operating plan reviews.[1] I've found that asking a set of core questions repeatedly produces several benefits. It forces your staff to anticipate issues and be prepared to respond to your questions. Along the way, you are implicitly instilling a thought process that helps people deal with critical implementation issues. Examples of such questions include, "What steps are required for the initiative's success: Number or quality of staff resources? Equipment? New information systems?" Or "How will this initiative affect other parts of the corporation? What support do we need from other areas across the company?" Over time, such questions train members of your organization so the implementation plans they create are more thoughtful and complete.

Identifying and Eliminating Obstacles to Execution

Assuming you've built a foundation for implementation within your team and have gradually shifted away from direct involvement in most of your team's priorities, you're in a position to take a fresh look at your organization. As you do, look for obstacles to implementation that crop up repeatedly and squander the energy of your team. Attacking flaws in work processes within your area or those that involve other groups within the company can pay big dividends. For example, in some companies, staff members may have to scramble all too often to respond to inaccurate forecasts of sales volume. If that's the case in your company, get the right people in the company involved to improve the sales forecasting process. As a general rule of thumb, as your team's ability to execute grows, you'll find you can add the greatest value in increasing your organization's capacity for implementation by identifying inefficient work processes and engaging your people to streamline them.

Realize that as you take steps to reduce your involvement in implementation at a detailed level, there will still be circumstances when you need to jump in. Even managers like Viv Campbell are prepared to get personally involved when major initiatives get off track. As you work to build your team's sense of ownership for implementation, it's important for people to know that you are prepared to reengage when circumstances call for it. And seasoned managers know that marketplace forces can put a wrinkle in their best-laid plans. For example, if another business unit in the company suffers a major profit shortfall, you may be called on to find ways to stimulate revenue or identify unplanned cost reductions. Such flexibility and resourcefulness are required of all executives. However, if you have been successful in creating a culture of implementation within your organization, you'll be better positioned to lead your team through such storms.

DISPLAYING UNUSED CAPACITY

The need to manage implementation never changes
regardless of how far you advance in your career. All
that changes is how you go about it. By delegating more
of the details and building your organization's capacity
for implementation, you'll be able to achieve the best
of both worlds: ensuring predictable execution and
demonstrating extra bandwidth, the capacity to take on
more responsibility. That sense of unused capacity not
only breeds confidence in those who make executive
promotion decisions. It also frees up your time to devote to
other core selection factors, such as leading innovation and
change within your organization.

CHAPTER 6

FACTOR 4
Exhibiting the Capacity for Innovation and Change

A few years ago I spoke with Brad Anderson, CEO of Best Buy at that time, about the qualities and skills he looked for when selecting the company's executives. In the course of that conversation, he said something I found provocative and profound: he looked for executives who had the wisdom to know when the organization needed to be fundamentally changed and shaken up and when the organization needed time to focus on incorporating prior changes. Lucien Alziari, the head of human resources for Avon Products, echoes Brad's point: "At Avon we need executives who can change how we do things—not simply manage the status quo."

Managing innovation and change has always been an important executive responsibility. However, in recent years the pace of technological, competitive, and marketplace change has increased the premium placed on executives who can lead innovation while still producing consistent and predictable results. To succeed at the C-suite level, an executive needs to demonstrate the ability to conceive of and lead the implementation of quantum-leap change. As a result, those who make decisions about promotions to the executive level look for evidence of the following. Can the individual

- Identify significant changes to existing ways of doing business in order to drive increased performance?
- Take necessary business and organizational risks—as opposed to playing it safe and sticking with tried-and-true solutions?
- Create an environment that fosters innovation and creative thinking throughout the organization?
- Push the organization out of its comfort zone when required—even if that prompts criticism on the part of those wedded to the status quo?

When they think of creativity and innovation, many managers immediately look to traditionally creative functions such as research and development, marketing, and product development. However, senior leaders like Brad Anderson and Lucien Alziari expect executives to lead innovation and change regardless of their role within the company—whether it's the creation of new strategies and business models, new information systems, the introduction of new organization structures, or new ways of working with customers. Successful executives don't have to be creative geniuses. But as you move up in the organization, you need the ability to form a team that includes creative thinkers who can help you generate new ideas and approaches. And to advance to the executive level, you'll need to demonstrate your ability to lead innovation and change when circumstances call for it.

The personal creativity of successful senior leaders varies considerably, as does how they go about introducing change within their organizations. Nevertheless, there are some important factors involved in managing innovation as illustrated by three very different managers: Danielle Williams, Tony Ferro, and Allen Gregory.

Danielle Williams

Danielle Williams was the manager of new product development for a large operating division of a global manufacturing enterprise. Since joining the company from a smaller competitor ten years before, Danielle had distinguished herself based on her creativity and drive. Over the years, she had spearheaded a number of new product initiatives that had helped the company leapfrog its competition and maintain its competitive edge.

Danielle had an interesting leadership style that contributed to her success as an innovator—but it also created some challenges for her team. Extremely focused on results, she was a risk taker who was not afraid to roll the dice on a new idea if it could help the company be first into the marketplace with a new product. She had developed an expansive and eclectic network of people within and outside the company she relied on to feed her creative juices. Danielle said she loved to connect the dots in new ways, and the people within her network gave her fresh ideas and insights—new dots—to connect. Her peers within the company marveled at her ability to pose big questions in novel ways. She framed questions in a manner that prompted new ways of looking at old problems and led to the generation of new product solutions.

As a manager, she was not hesitant about challenging her team to find ways to implement her product ideas. She often said that organizational structure and processes were only a means to an end in pushing new ideas forward, and she was never one to rest on her laurels and become complacent. Early in her career, she had had great success with certain product concepts and approaches to new product development. As the business grew and new opportunities emerged, she wasn't wedded to how things had been done in the past. Instead, she was prepared to create new methods—even if that meant departing from the source of her past success.

When members of Danielle's team heard that she was excited about a new concept, they would fasten their seat belts. Once she had decided on a new product idea, she could be expected to pursue it aggressively. Danielle's peers and executives at the company who knew her well, however, noticed something unusual about Danielle's approach. Although she was hugely creative, Danielle was the source of virtually all the innovative ideas that emerged from her team. She was wide ranging in her thought process and open to ideas from a variety of sources, but when her staff members came forward with new ideas, she tended to steamroll them. So over time, her team came to be composed of very capable and very organized lieutenants who were skilled at implementing her ideas.

This pattern was the focus of discussion during annual succession planning meetings. There was no question that Danielle was a valuable idea generator whose ideas could help the company grow. However, more senior leadership positions in new product development and in research and development required managing large numbers of staff. The company's future plans called for an increased level of investment in new product development to drive growth and reestablish the company's position as an innovator within the industry. As senior executives talked about Danielle's future, their major question was whether she could operate as a leader of a large group and cultivate the creativity of others—distinct from her own—and create a climate where strong, innovative people could flourish.

Tony Ferro

Tony Ferro was the manager of sales and fulfillment for a large, well-known catalogue retailer. He and his team were responsible for a number of activities within the company that included taking customer orders and putting them into the company's fulfillment system so they could be assembled, packaged, and shipped, along with accurate customer invoices. Tony was an ambitious manager who wanted to continue to grow within the company. As a result, he was pleased to be selected to participate in the company's career development program for high-potential managers. As part of that program, I assessed Tony's leadership skills and provided him with feedback.

Three years before, after rising through the company's ranks, Tony had been promoted to the position of fulfillment manager. His work ethic was legendary. He had a reputation for being a strong leader who possessed great values and knew how to rally the troops to attack operational problems. Tony also had a deep understanding of his organization's performance levers: the activities that had the biggest impact on results. The implementation of new initiatives in Tony's department was well-nigh flawless. Performance measures and follow-up procedures were in place so the department operated like clockwork.

Members of the company's senior executive group, however, were aware of some troubling signs. Although Tony had brought in some staff at lower levels within the department, his team of direct reports was composed of staff members he had known and worked with for many years. Sometimes referred to by others within the company as a "good-old-boy" network, it was a team he felt comfortable with. When performance review time rolled around each year, Tony's salary increase recommendations tended to be about the same for each direct report. He believed that if all team members were pulling their own weight, it was better to reward people equally and avoid harming team morale.

Like Tony, the majority of his team members had been with the company for many years, and they were all committed to the company's success. However, the group tended to be inwardly focused. Neither Tony nor members of his team devoted much time to exploring new practices outside the company, and they rarely engaged in benchmarking conversations with other companies within or outside the industry.

Tony and his team members had a well-defined process to plan and follow up on new initiatives. However, it was focused on the short term and not much time was devoted to long-range planning or blue-sky thinking. During the team's planning sessions, there was a tendency for discussion to get to the tactical level quickly. Tony and his team had done a commendable job of improving the systems and processes by which the department operated. However, at no point did Tony encourage a fresh look at how work was done within the organization or schedule time to consider what changes might be required from a longer-term perspective.

During their succession planning discussions, the senior leaders discussed whether Tony was ready to move up a level to the vice president of operations, where he would be responsible for all of the company's operational functions: fulfillment, sales, logistics, and information technology. Initially there was a lot of support for promoting Tony into this role: he was a proven performer and a strong, well-liked leader, and he lived the company's values. However, after extensive discussion, the group of senior executives turned lukewarm about promoting him into such a role.

Although the company had been very successful of late, aggressive new competitors were entering the industry, and customers were changing their buying behavior as they became more comfortable with online shopping. There was no question that Tony could motivate an organization and manage incremental improvement in performance. The larger issue for the executives was whether he and his team could envision fundamentally different ways to support the continued growth of the business in the face of the marketplace changes that were rapidly becoming apparent. They knew that Tony had strong personal relationships with many members of his team and others within the organization. Was he prepared to challenge and push his group toward new ways of doing business—especially if he encountered resistance from team members who had become comfortable operating within the existing system?

The senior executives ultimately concluded that Tony was a valuable employee who could enjoy a long and productive career with the company. However, when the position of vice president of operations opened up, they decided to bring in an external candidate who could take a fresh look at the company's operations—a decision that was a blow to Tony.

Allen Gregory

I got to know Allen Gregory in the course of my long-standing relationship with his company, a large financial services firm, and had a chance to work with him directly when he took over as general manager of one of the company's business units. Allen would be the first to tell you that he wasn't the most creative manager in the company. However, he had an impressive track record for introducing innovation in several assignments and had demonstrated the ability to drive change within an organization.

When he became general manager, his business unit was facing some significant challenges. After a number of years of success, recent industry changes had severely depressed the unit's performance—as well as morale

117

within the organization. One of the reasons Allen was put into the GM role was that he was an accomplished change manager. He also had a strong product development background, so he quickly went to work with the product development staff to reenergize that area. Although he devoted a good deal of time and energy to product development, he set an expectation within his team that every part of the unit needed change.

A few months after taking over as general manager of the unit, Allen had made changes to his organization structure and team. Based on his early evaluation of the business unit, he had determined that the existing organization structure was impeding the level of customer focus he felt was needed. He brought in a couple of new team members whom he knew to be creative and change oriented, and he modified the roles of several direct reports. Beyond strengthening the team and streamlining the unit's organization structure, he wanted to send a message to his entire unit that change was on the way.

Allen was comfortable surrounding himself with strong players, including those more creative than himself and those who knew the business better than he did. He was open to new ideas regardless of the source. Although action and results oriented, he had the patience to let new ideas percolate for a while in the belief that people in his organization could take the kernel of a new idea and improve on it. Although quite competitive, Allen didn't think that every new idea or initiative had to succeed. He was prepared to test new ideas and then either invest in the most promising ones or pull the plug on those unlikely to succeed. Most important, he was highly resilient. He told his staff not to worry about seemingly well-thought-through ideas that didn't pan out. "Some things work out, some don't," he said. The important thing, he argued, was to try new things: to see which ideas succeeded and to learn something useful from those that didn't.

Shortly after forming his new team, he scheduled a number of planning and brainstorming meetings to create a sense of energy about innovation within the team. He looked for every opportunity to communicate his case for change to his entire organization and explain why the status quo was not sustainable. In meetings with his team, he encouraged off-the-wall thinking and challenged his team to redefine the questions it posed since he believed that asking the right questions—and phrasing questions in new and provocative ways—was often the first step in innovative thinking.

In the course of his team's planning discussion, Allen made sure that the team considered the larger corporate organization. What impact would the team's proposed initiatives have on other units within the company? Conversely, what support was needed from other parts of the corporation for new initiatives to succeed? Resources from corporate engineering? The creation of new financial tools by the corporate finance department?

There were times when Allen would drive his team crazy by pushing for change when not everything was nailed down fully in the team's implementation plans. He was concerned about getting bogged down and expressed confidence that his team members would sort things out as new initiatives were introduced. As his team started to come together, Allen began to shift to a more hands-off approach to managing the day-to-day work. He also spent a considerable amount of time reviewing staff members' performance and making salary and bonus recommendations. He wanted to recognize the innovators—including those who took risks and failed.

It took the better part of a year, but his organization became comfortable with Allen's style. The unit's performance bounced back, and his organization came to appreciate the benefits of his management approach. After two years in his job, he was promoted to lead another business unit within the company, one that needed a large dose of innovation and change.

CREATIVITY VERSUS MANAGING INNOVATION

The case of Danielle Williams illustrates an important and useful distinction between creativity and innovation—one that's helpful if you'd like to develop your skills in this area. Creativity is an individual's ability to generate breakthrough ideas. By contrast, innovation is the ability to foster an environment that brings forth the creativity of others. Creativity is a wonderful quality for any manager to have. However, a high level of personal creativity, while certainly useful, is only a nice-to-have factor when it comes to executive promotion decisions. The crucial skill is the demonstrated ability to stimulate innovation and lead change within the organization.

As in the case with strategic thinking ability discussed in Chapter Three, the bar for innovation and change management is typically set higher for managers in business unit leadership positions and departments such as marketing, product development, and research and development than for managers in other areas. However, given the pace of change in most industries, the ability to guide the identification and introduction of new innovations is important for leaders in all areas, including manufacturing, information technology, and finance. At one time, continuous improvement—the constant refinement of existing ways of doing business that yielded incremental performance improvement—was enough. Now companies look for executives who can work with their teams to identify breakthrough solutions and introduce large-scale change.

There's an ongoing debate about whether creative ability can be developed. Some management thinkers, like David Kord Murray, an innovator and author of *Borrowing Brilliance*, and Clayton Christensen, Jeffrey Dyer, and Hal Gregersen, authors of the *Harvard Business Review* article, "The Innovator's DNA," claim that it can be.[1] Whether or not that's true, in my experience the ability to manage innovation and change can be developed—assuming you take the time to understand what's involved in the creative process and master the techniques of innovation and change management. So, to develop your skills in this area, investigate how innovators operate, and then incorporate as many of their techniques as possible into your leadership approach.

To get started, it's useful to study truly innovative leaders: people like Michael Dell of Dell, the computer and technology company; Herb Kelleher and the other founders of Southwest Airlines; Jeff Bezos and Amazon, the Internet retailing sensation; and the leaders of Sony who, a generation ago, introduced the Walkman, the first portable music player. The specifics of how such creative people identified and developed innovative ideas vary considerably. Nonetheless, there are important commonalities in the way creative people think and manage the process of innovation: the ability to look at things differently, experiment, and foster a risk-taking mentality, and a willingness to challenge the organization in the interest of change.

Looking at Things in New Ways

Creative people are able to see problems and opportunities differently from others and, by definition, generate new solutions. They frequently start by thinking deeply about customers' underlying needs—not just those that customers can express in surveys or focus groups. A classic example is the Sony Walkman. What music lover in the late 1970s could have told a market researcher about her desire for a compact, portable music player, something inconceivable to most people at the time?

Highly creative people are masters of asking big, stimulating questions and framing them in ways that prompt fresh thinking. They ask, "Why?" "Why not?" "What if?" and "How might we . . . ?" questions. Like Danielle Williams, they have an almost uncanny ability to connect seemingly unrelated bits of information in order to generate a new idea or approach. To do so, they expand their range of information sources and are alert to analogies—often from different industries or fields of study—that can be applied to a situation they're dealing with. According to David Kord Murray, a basic building block of successful innovators is borrowing ideas from others: competitors, other industries, or even the scientific, arts, or entertainment sectors. For example, a team at a fast-growing philanthropic organization I know was given the task of creating a new organizational model. Rather than benchmark with other nonprofits, they spent time with research laboratories and public relations firms in order to think creatively about ways to organize their staff.

If you're seeking to display a greater ability to manage innovation, make sure you have a sufficient number of creative people on your team—staff who are open to change and capable of generating new ideas. Depending on your organization's need for innovation, think through whether you have the right mix of highly creative people, strong implementers, and those knowledgeable about the company who can test new ideas. Factor those conclusions into your plan to upgrade your team.

Next, consider ways to expand your network and gain access to new and different sources of information. For most of us, it's a natural human tendency to gravitate toward people who share the same experiences and opinions that we do. Instead, take steps to locate people inside and outside your company who bring different knowledge and perspectives—people who can stimulate your creative thinking and act as sounding boards for new ideas. Find out what they're reading and thinking about in the interest of identifying new concepts you can introduce to your team. Try to avoid the tendency of managers like Tony Ferro who become overly focused on what their companies are doing today. As part of your team's planning, identify a range of companies and new practices to research. Such benchmarking, especially if it is combined with direct customer interaction, can be useful in prompting your team to conceive of new ways of doing business.

Brainstorming and Experimentation

Highly creative people are not necessarily any less practical than others. However, they tend to be comfortable with ambiguity and enjoy brainstorming: generating lots of ideas in a free-flowing way. Before deciding on a course of action, they create multiple options and are prepared to prolong the time window before judging and selecting which idea to pursue. During this period, they are open to seeing how alternatives may combine and morph into new and better options to solve a problem.

As they move beyond idea generation, they devise ways to test the most promising options to see which are worthy of being pursued. Creative people tend to be reasonably comfortable with the messiness of innovation and the fact that things may turn out differently than planned. Often the experience gained during the experimentation phase causes the innovation to be refined and redirected into, new areas. One classic example is 3M's development of Post-it notes. Although the formula for the adhesive was initially considered a failure, staff at 3M saw its potential for low-adhesion uses, and a multimillion-dollar product was born.

Give thought to how your team plans for the future and how often you get your people together for blue-sky thinking sessions. Too often corporate planning processes focus managers' attention on next year's targets and budgets—thus reinforcing short-term thinking and emphasis on incremental improvement. Schedule opportunities for members of your team to ideate: to pose and discuss new, provocative questions and generate multiple options to change the status quo. Make sure you build in the time required for new ideas to develop and allow people to modify or combine new alternatives, thus turning them into truly productive ideas.

As potentially valuable ideas emerge, look for ways to test and learn from them. A pilot project in one part of the organization is one typical approach. If you and your team launch a pilot, be clear about what you hope to learn from the test. That way, you can increase the investment—in dollars and other resources—in ideas that show promise and terminate work on those that don't work out as planned. Whatever approach you use, build in time to learn from your experiments, because what you take away from a test may be invaluable in finding future solutions.

Encouraging Risk Taking

By definition, innovation and change involve risk, and creative people tend to be comfortable with risk—and the consequent possibility of failure. I once worked with a highly creative manager who posted a sign in his office that read: "Remember, Babe Ruth struck out 1,330 times." He wanted to remind himself and his team that even the famous baseball slugger had nearly twice as many strikeouts as home runs and that the willingness to fail is required to hit a home run with an innovative idea. As a result, creative people adopt the attitude that failure isn't failure if it leads to an insight that's useful in finding the next creative idea.

Innovators get bored with the status quo and repetitive activity. Once a new idea or approach has been launched successfully, they set off on a search for the next big idea. In some cases, the next innovation requires them to move beyond approaches that have worked in the past, even those that have defined their success, to create the next innovation. This is a phenomenon an executive I know once labeled "destroying your own monuments" in the interest of change and progress.

Depending on your company's culture, one of the hardest things to do is promote risk taking within your team. Some companies, like 3M, have worked hard over the years to create cultures that encourage people to take risks. In more risk-averse companies, the perceived penalties for failure far outweigh the perceived benefits. As a result, people tend not to stick their necks out to support change and feel more comfortable operating within the tried and true. In such companies, more time is spent trying to assess blame when things don't work out as planned than in rewarding those who took reasonable and calculated risks.

I've seen companies employ a variety of techniques to counteract this phenomenon. Some years ago, Citibank (before it became part of Citigroup) had a tradition: the No Guts, No Glory award. This award was presented publicly, often in a jocular tone, and was intended to recognize someone who had failed while taking a calculated risk—and to encourage risk taking on the part of others. Another useful approach to promoting risk taking is the after-action review, a process designed to identify lessons learned. Developed by the U.S. Army some years ago, an after-action review is just that: a structured discussion after a new initiative has been completed to determine what worked, what didn't work, and what important lessons can be gleaned from the effort. Over time a focus on lessons learned—as opposed to who screwed up—will encourage a higher level of risk taking within your team.

As you consider how to encourage risk taking and innovation within your team, look for ways to provide disproportionate rewards for those who succeed in identifying and implementing new innovations. When everyone on the team gets pretty much the same reward, as was the case on Tony Ferro's team, it can reinforce people's tendency to play it safe—since there is so little upside if you take a risk and succeed.

Pushing the Organizational Envelope

At the same time they push themselves intellectually in pursuit of a new idea, innovators are prepared to push their organizations out of their comfort zones: to challenge them to move beyond the status quo, however familiar and comfortable it may be. That's really the point Brad Anderson of Best Buy made to me: in order to continue to grow, organizations periodically need to be stretched and challenged to avoid complacency. Creative leaders typically see opportunities and challenges before others in the company do, especially when things are going well. As a result, they are prepared to launch a new innovation even if the details of implementation are not fully worked through, confident that their people can figure it out and make the necessary course corrections. In the process they're willing to accept push-back from the naysayers and those wedded to the status quo. Although they listen carefully for important issues that could derail the success of the new initiative, innovators are prepared·to live with some degree of organizational angst as the company learns to incorporate the change they believe is vital for continued success. Especially in well-established companies, this involves your ability to exercise managerial courage: the courage of your convictions along with some thick skin when others criticize your desire for change.

IT'S ALL ABOUT ATTITUDE

Keep in mind that one important aspect of change, risk taking, is both attitudinal and emotional. At its core, risk taking demands a willingness to try something new and fail. As I've worked with executives and high-potential managers over the years, a fear of making mistakes—what I call the perfect paper syndrome—is often the biggest obstacle to success in this area.

If you struggle with taking the risk required for real innovation, I have two recommendations. The first is to start small and build up your comfort level. Begin with new ideas and initiatives that pose relatively small amounts of risk, but challenge yourself to pursue them faster and more creatively than you might otherwise be inclined. Keep working to increase your risk tolerance so you'll be prepared to take bigger risks on bigger initiatives in the future. My second suggestion goes back to the sign that reminded my friend and his team that Babe Ruth struck out 1,330 times. When a potential innovation emerges—one that entails risk but could move the needle in terms of growth or performance—do your homework. Determine the downside, and create a contingency plan: what you'll do if things don't work out as planned. And then swing for the fences and try to hit the ball out of the park.

As you review the skills needed to develop your ability to lead innovation within your organization, keep one final point in mind: any significant change in your area in all likelihood will either affect or demand support from others in the company. Therefore, leading change successfully also requires you to display lateral management skills—the ability to work effectively with others across organizational lines. That's the topic of the next chapter.

CHAPTER 7

FACTOR 5

Working Across Organizational Boundaries

Teamwork. Collaboration. A management team characterized by one for all and all for one. That's a laudable goal, and one that many companies set for their executive teams, but it's rarely accomplished by the great majority of them. Rather, leadership teams are usually characterized by some degree of internal tension arising from two main sources: the leaders' personal ambitions and the competing objectives of different groups that in most organizations lead to friction between executives. In this environment of inherent tension, some managers, especially those not skilled in working with others, speak derisively about the need to "play nicely" with their peers and coworkers. Those who say this, however, often misunderstand why the ability to collaborate is a critical skill. It's not a question of teamwork for teamwork's sake. Rather, it relates to an executive's ability to work across organization lines to get things accomplished.

Organizational cultures differ significantly in their willingness to accept—or in some cases encourage—competition within their organizations. Some companies attempt to foster collegiality among their executives, while others stimulate competition in hopes of increased performance and creativity. Whatever value your company places on collaboration, recognize that the ability to work productively with others across organizational lines—what I call lateral management—continues to grow in importance in most companies for a number of reasons: the popularity of matrix-type organization structures (where people report to two or even more managers), the growing prevalence of joint ventures and business alliances, the proliferation of centralized groups that provide service to multiple parts of the organization, and the need to drive change quickly across the organization. As a result, those who make decisions about promotions to the executive level look for answers to the following questions. Can the individual

- Build positive working relationships with peers and coworkers and exercise the influence, persuasion, and negotiation skills required to get work done across organization borders?

132

- Demonstrate an understanding of how the organization operates and how decisions are made in order to gain support for her positions?

- Demonstrate an understanding of other groups' goals and objectives and anticipate the impact that new strategies and initiatives will have on peers and their organizations?

- Manage conflict by addressing rather than avoiding it; working with others to resolve it; and achieving, if at all possible, mutually acceptable solutions?

Some managers are more naturally team oriented than others, and some have better interpersonal skills. However, several important skills underlie the ability to get work done across organizational boundaries—as illustrated by the cases of Allison James and Fred Henderson.

Allison James

The head of a small business unit of a rapidly growing technology company, Allison James was all about speed and getting results. Before joining the company six years ago, she had graduated from a top business school and then had spent three years with a prestigious consulting firm. She was known for her outstanding analytical skills and ability to get to the root of virtually any business problem. She was especially skilled in dealing with turnaround situations.

She loved the challenge of parachuting into a troubled business with the mandate to make the changes required for the unit to regain profitability.

Since joining the company, she had been rewarded handsomely for her efforts, and promotions had come her way quickly. But some managers complained about her sharp elbows. Allison was the first to admit that she had little time or patience for hand holding with peers in other departments, and she abhorred organizational politics. To her, time spent with peers was time better spent analyzing the business, creating action plans, and making things happen. She saw her peers as stodgy, risk averse, and given to endless debates. If her coworkers could adopt her drive and sense of urgency, she believed, the company would be a lot better off.

Her peers painted a picture of Allison that was quite different. Although she was widely respected for her business acumen and ability to produce results, Allison's peers complained that they were routinely blindsided by decisions she and her team made that had negative impacts on their areas. She was described as a poor listener who became locked into her position and was not open to considering another person's recommendation or point of view. Several times over the past few years, Allison and her peers had disagreed about the best course of action. According to her peers, rather than deal with them directly to resolve the issue, she would end-run them by going to her boss to get her position endorsed. She almost always got her recommendation approved, making her peers scramble to achieve their own departmental objectives. Not surprisingly, this behavior generated ill feelings on the part of peers. They tried to explain to Allison the consequences of her proposed actions on their areas and offered to find alternative ways for Allison's unit to accomplish its goals. However, they ran into Allison's my-way-or-the-highway approach and came away feeling that their concerns hadn't been acknowledged, let alone addressed.

Increasingly, Allison's management style was creating a dilemma for members of the company's senior management team. There was no question that she was a top performer who could be counted on to deliver on almost any objective. However, promoting her to the next level meant that she would manage some of her current peers—a move that might cause an insurrection within the organization. Besides, at a more senior level within the organization, Allison would have to interact to an even greater extent with different groups across the company—so the complaints heard from peer organizations were likely to get worse rather than better. Unless she could make a significant change in her approach to working with peers, it appeared that Allison would be offered a series of turnaround assignments but never make it to the executive level.

Fred Henderson

Radiant Technologies, a global manufacturing corporation, hired Fred four years ago to reinvigorate its research and development department. Radiant's CEO had recognized that a number of the company's core products were increasingly outdated and beginning to lose market share. Since Fred had come from a company with a well-deserved reputation for product innovation, his arrival at Radiant was greeted with some fanfare.

Radiant Technologies was a stable, well-managed organization with a reputation for high quality in everything it did. The company culture was characterized by a high level of collegiality. In fact, a majority of the senior managers had been with the company for most of their careers and routinely talked about their time spent together in the trenches over the years. Many of the company's business unit heads were located in regional offices around the world and were afforded significant freedom to run their operations. The implicit cultural norm at Radiant Technologies was, "Do what's right for the customer and the business." As one senior executive said, "It's usually better if we take our time and make sure plans are well thought out rather than try to be fast and risk making a mistake."

Fred was one of the few outsiders who had been brought in at his level in the company's history. There was no question that he had created a new sense of energy within the research function and had built a strong department team. Although he was highly respected and well liked personally, some grumbling from peers led Fred's manager to ask me to work with him as a coach. It turns out that these peers' concerns were not at all trivial. In addition to revitalizing the R&D effort, Fred had been recruited in hopes that he could fill an executive-level slot in the future. But emerging peer relationship issues were calling future promotion into question.

As is often the case, I started my work with Fred by gathering some data that included a series of confidential interviews with his boss and his peers. The results were surprisingly consistent. Those interviewed were confident that Fred could add tremendous value to the company. He knew his stuff and was strategic, highly innovative, results oriented, and prepared to take calculated risks to drive the business. At the same time, his peers felt that they were not adequately consulted when Fred and his team members developed plans for major R&D projects.

Fred tended to sell upper management on his new programs and then race to get them implemented. In the process, he usually didn't involve peers in any meaningful way. They claimed that they would be informed about a new initiative early on in the planning phase. However, they were frequently surprised by changes to the project plan when it was ready to be implemented. For all of his terrific abilities, Fred seemed to be tone-deaf to the company culture, especially the need to develop support from others within the various business units.

Fred's boss admitted that he had tried to communicate these issues to Fred but had held back on being totally candid. Since there was so much riding on the development of new products, he didn't want to stifle the creativity and drive Fred brought to the R&D effort.

Fred was keenly interested in the results of my interviews. In fact, his peers' feedback didn't come as a total shock to him. He had been aware of some concerns and felt he had been unsuccessful in becoming a member of the fraternity of managers who'd been with the company for many years. Still, the premium the company placed on getting everyone onboard with new initiatives came as a surprise to him. As we began to talk about how he could build relationships and generate support for his key projects, his greatest concern was that he would lose his drive for innovation and have to spend his time in prolonged meetings.

That concern notwithstanding, Fred was highly motivated to succeed and took aggressive steps to deal with the feedback. I asked him if he had a new initiative in the R&D pipeline that would provide him with an opportunity to collaborate with peers. As luck would have it, he and his staff had begun putting together preliminary plans for a project that would draw in most of the company's business units and several corporate staff groups as well. Based on our discussions, Fred and his team scheduled meetings to review the preliminary plans with a number of business unit heads. The R&D staff modified its initial plans based on ideas provided by the business unit leaders, and Fred went out of his way to demonstrate to others how their feedback had been factored into the final project plan. Given the company's global reach, he scheduled several international trips over the next six months. During these visits to regional office locations around the world, he met with his peers and their teams. In each meeting, he showed a sincere interest in understanding their business priorities and the marketplace situations they faced.

Fred asked me to follow up on his efforts by interviewing a number of his peers six months later. It was clear from these discussions that there had been a substantial turnaround in terms of how his peers viewed him as a collaborator. He was still seen as a valued, results-oriented manager. However, he was now given high marks for his efforts to engage and involve others. As one peer said, "He finally gets the fact that even though senior management may say 'go' to something he wants to do, it's still necessary to get the support of people across the organization before moving out."

I asked Fred whether the steps he had taken to change others' opinions had caused him to lose his focus on innovation or get bogged down in endless peer meetings. He laughed and said they hadn't. What had changed was the time he devoted to communicating with peers: working to understand their objectives, getting their input, and

139

trying to respond in a meaningful way. He even reported that the quality of his initiatives had improved due to the input he had received from peers. Although in some cases the planning phase for some of the projects took longer than before, he was confident that initiatives were being implemented faster and more efficiently due to the widespread understanding and support that had been achieved.

Clearly Fred's progress in building peer relationships was impressive. Given the strength of the company's grapevine, Radiant's CEO heard this feedback directly from several of Fred's peers. As a result, Fred was listed as a candidate to take on additional responsibilities when the company updated its executive succession plan.

DEVELOPING LATERAL MANAGEMENT ABILITY

In the course of my coaching with executives, I frequently work with people on their collaboration and peer relationship skills. Like Allison James, some executives bemoan the time required to build relationships with managers across the company and secure support for their plans and initiatives. Without a doubt, in some companies this can be arduous and time-consuming. But these executives miss a fundamental point: the time an executive spends working with and through others to get work done isn't time spent away from doing his job. It *is* his job.

Just as meeting with customers, managing suppliers, dealing with regulators, or cultivating potential investors is central to an executive's work, interacting with peers across the organization is a fundamental task of executive leadership. What makes it uncomfortable for many managers is that it involves influencing without direct authority. In order to be able to get work done across organizational lines within your company, you'll need to hone your skills in four key areas: forging positive working relationships with a wide range of people; displaying an understanding of how organizations work operationally, politically, and culturally; influencing and persuading others to get support for your initiatives; and dealing effectively with conflict, which is a fact of life in any organization.

Building Positive Working Relationships

The ability to work across organizational lines begins with developing relationships with peers and other coworkers important to your success. Many managers misconstrue this advice and think I'm encouraging them to make friends with their peers. That's beside the point. In some cases, I've seen members of executive teams become real friends on a personal level. More often, though, the relationship is all business, and the executives have little or no interaction outside work. Rather than thinking about developing friendships with peers, focus your efforts on building positive working relationships based on trust.

Such relationships not only help in communicating
with others; they also give you what I call the handholds
required to influence and persuade others. Trust-based
relationships provide a foundation for you to work
through miscommunications and differences of opinion
with others when they crop up. People who trust you
aren't likely to question your motives before they've
taken the time to fully understand the situation
at hand.

As a starting point for developing a positive working
relationship with a colleague, consider the following
questions:

- What do you know about the other person's personal
  goals, values, motivations, even interests and
  hobbies?

- What are her business objectives, and how can you
  and your organization provide help in achieving
  them?

- How does she tend to make decisions? For example, is
  she highly analytical and therefore requires that
  proposed decisions be supported by detail and data—or
  is a persuasive argument sufficient?

- Who is she likely to consult in making a decision?

- Whose opinion does she respect? If certain people
  within the organization support a particular position, is
  she likely to get onboard with it?

Collectively, the answers to these questions provide you with the handholds necessary to influence and persuade others.

Taking time to probe a peer's goals, values, and interests will help you find personal points of connection and begin to build a relationship. In his article, "Harnessing the Science of Persuasion," Robert Cialdini, an expert on influence, writes about the importance of finding common interests and affinities as a way to begin building trust and goodwill.[1] Not surprisingly, peers will be predisposed to support you and your initiatives if they like and respect you—and more inclined to try to thwart you if they don't.

Allison James would dismiss all of this as psychology and a waste of effort. The only time she spent with her peers and other coworkers was when she and her team wanted them to agree to support her team's plans. As a result, she had little insight into what made her peers tick and never got off the ground in building relationships with them. Worse, her uncompromising approach tended to stimulate resentment and resistance on the part of others.

Developing Organizational and Political Understanding

Finding common interests and some personal chemistry with others is an important starting point. From there you need to demonstrate your organizational savvy, that is, a fundamental understanding of how the organization works, in two ways. The first is more straightforward but can take years to master: how the business operates and how the different parts of the organization interact with one another to produce results. Knowing this helps you anticipate the impact of decisions on the various parts of the organization. This perspective allows you to make better decisions and helps you know whether your proposed plans and initiatives will contribute to or impede your peers' ability to accomplish their objectives. For example, your recommendation to reduce staff in the customer service department may streamline operations and reduce cost. However, you'd better be in contact with the sales force to make sure it doesn't have a negative impact on their ability to service existing customers and sell to new ones.

If you develop a reputation for trying to advance a new project without having anticipated the impact on other parts of the organization, in all likelihood you'll meet with resistance from your peers and their staff. Worse, your company's senior executives are likely to conclude that you have a limited perspective on the business and are prone to making half-baked decisions harmful to the business. Keep in mind the dangers of being pegged as a manager with a narrow, parochial perspective on the business and the organization—one of the deselector factors described in Chapter One.

The second component of organization savvy is developing an understanding of how decisions get made and how to get your proposed initiatives approved. For many managers, this is the greater challenge of the two since in many companies, decision-making processes are not clearly defined. Sometimes new decisions will be made relatively clear-cut, for example, how projects will be reviewed and approved when the annual budget is developed. Often, however, the decision-making process may be somewhat obscure, especially if it involves a large initiative that impacts several organizational units. Who makes the ultimate call? A single executive? The senior management committee? Whose opinion weighs most heavily in the final decision? What criteria will be used to make the decision?

To maximize support for their proposals, successful executives take time to address questions such as these. In doing so, they work with their teams to create two parallel plans: a thorough plan outlining the details of the proposed initiative and an endorsement plan that sets out the specific steps they and their team members will take to generate support on the part of the key decision makers. As you create your plan to gain approval for a major initiative, approach your boss to get her sense of the decision-making process that will be employed. Recognize that organizational politics can be very fluid as executives' roles and decision-making influence shift—often in ways that aren't obvious to many managers. Be as creative as possible in identifying those who can help decipher your company's decision-making landscape. Your best source may be your boss's boss, someone you worked for in the past, or a well-connected peer who has his finger on the pulse of the organization.

Influencing and Persuading Others

Your endorsement plan should be focused on the key decision makers and those whose opinions they respect. As you craft your plan, consider a number of important questions:

- Who has a vested interest in the success or failure of your recommended plan?
- Are they predisposed to act favorably or negatively to your plan—or are they likely to be neutral and less involved?
- Will they have to provide resources (dollars, staff, systems support and so forth) to support the plan? Or is their concurrence sufficient?
- Do they view you as someone who's reliable and can execute the plan—or do you need to take steps to increase your credibility as someone who can deliver the results promised?

As you develop your plan, be aware of several simple and straightforward principles of human behavior that people like Allison James often neglect in their rush to get their initiatives approved. Keep in mind that people are more likely to support an idea or plan if

- They feel they've had meaningful input into the design of the plan and believe they will share in the credit if the idea is successful.

- They feel they've been listened to, with their opinions and concerns acknowledged and, to the extent possible, addressed.

- You have actively supported them in the past or they are confident you will do so in the future. (This is Robert Cialdini's reciprocity—or give-and-get—principle.)

- Other people whose opinions they trust support the idea.

- They are confident that information about the plan has been fully disclosed—and that they won't be tricked or blindsided if they support the idea.

If you have already taken steps to build positive working relationships with your peers and coworkers, you'll have insight into their goals and objectives, both business and personal. You'll also have a sense of their values, motivation, and interests. Armed with this information and keeping these rules of human behavior in mind, you're in a position to implement your endorsement plan.

This typically includes conducting briefings with the key decision makers in advance of meetings where your proposed initiative will be presented and, you hope, approved. In these briefings, don't simply attempt to sell the other person on your recommended plan. Take the time to tease out her questions, concerns, and level of support. Pay special attention to her suggestions about reviewing your proposal with others ("Have you run this by ...?"). She may be alerting you to another person or group whose support you'll need for your plan to be approved. In addition, the people she recommends you contact may be her "influencers": others within the organization she is likely to consult with before making a final decision.

Executives in most organizations are involved in a wide range of issues, and they don't have time to dig deeply into every one. As a result, they often turn to trusted staff whose expertise and judgment they rely on. In the course of these briefings, try to find areas where you can provide support or resources to the other person in achieving her objectives (Cialdini's reciprocity principle).

As you consider ways to encourage others to support your initiatives, recall the steps that Fred Henderson pursued. In meetings, he not only communicated his new plans but solicited others' ideas. He was careful not to compromise the most critical aspects of his plans, but he included his peers' suggestions whenever possible to improve the quality of the final proposal and increase their sense of ownership. Importantly, he and his team committed to communication with others involved in their projects. As circumstances changed, Fred was quick to inform those who would be affected by the changes. Such communication served to increase Fred's level of trust and credibility with his peers and contributed to getting their support.

Addressing and Resolving Conflict

Companies differ significantly in the level of competition they will accept (or in some cases promote!) compared to the premium placed on collaboration and teamwork. Regardless of where your company lies on that spectrum, to be a prime candidate to move to the C suite, you'll need to demonstrate your ability to manage conflict since strong differences of opinion and friction between units crop up from time to time in any organization. Contention in organizations takes many forms: disagreements about the best business strategy to pursue, whether to make an acquisition, whose growth investment to fund, or whether to move a talented staff member to a new position in another part of the organization. The question isn't whether there will be conflict in your company. The question is how effective you'll be in addressing differences of opinion when they occur. Although some companies are more comfortable with conflict than others, intense and unresolved conflict ultimately takes too much time and saps too much organizational energy to be tolerated. That's the situation that executives at Allison James's company faced in dealing with a top performer who had burned too many bridges with others along the way.

Successfully managing conflict has two main dimensions: stepping up to address the conflict—as opposed to avoiding it and letting it fester—and having the skills to resolve it if at all possible. Prudent executives pick their battles and are careful to choose the right time to address a conflict situation. However, a consistent tendency to avoid conflict will reduce your credibility. Others will paint you as someone uncomfortable dealing with difficult situations and making tough, unpopular decisions when called for.

Once they get over the hurdle of engaging with others in a conflict situation, I see too many managers who are poorly equipped to deal with the strong disagreements involved. The result is the proverbial blood on the floor. Too often each party gets locked into his own position. An unyielding, overly competitive approach tends to harden the battle lines and make any resolution difficult, if not impossible, to achieve. Don't get me wrong. I'm not suggesting you roll over and simply accept the other person's position or agree to a compromise solution that's not right for the business. What I do advise is that you take the time to understand the other person's position and, more important, his overriding objectives. Look beyond the position the other party is advocating. What goal is he really trying to accomplish? Knowing that allows you both to be creative in attempting to find solutions that accomplish each others' goals.

In their book *Getting to Yes*, Roger Fisher, William Ury, and Bruce Patton suggest that you and the other person articulate your real objectives as a starting point for generating new alternatives that might represent a mutually acceptable solution.[2] While still holding fast to the things you believe are critical to the solution, look for elements of your position that are less important and that you can concede. Often (but not always) demonstrating some flexibility and acknowledging the merits of the other person's position can break a logjam and help move toward a solution that both of you can support. These conversations aren't easy, but the benefits to your relationships with peers can be significant once your colleagues recognize your skill in working through and resolving differences of opinion. Demonstrating your ability to navigate potential gridlock situations will contribute to your reputation for lateral management and make it easier for you to work across organizational lines in the future.

It's important to add one caveat here. The approaches I've described to build relationships with peers, resolve conflict, and ultimately get work done across the organization aren't foolproof. On occasion, you and the other person will simply have to agree to disagree. There will also likely be times when you run into a peer, a truly competitive alley fighter, who seems immune to collaboration. I suggest that you start off by trying to engage the other person to understand her goals and objectives and then attempt to work toward mutually acceptable solutions. You may be pleasantly surprised that in this way, you're able to develop an acceptable working relationship—that by displaying trust and a willingness to collaborate, the other person will respond in kind. If this doesn't happen, make sure to inform your manager of your efforts and the response you're getting from the other party. Your manager may have ideas about ways to deal with the situation or offer to help achieve resolution. In any event, by taking the proper steps and demonstrating your desire to be a team player, the other person—and not you—eventually will get pegged within the organization as the one who's parochial and noncollaborative.

DEVELOPING YOUR INFLUENCE AND IMPACT

Over time a manager's level of influence within a company can increase based on a number of factors, not all of which relate to organizational level. The techniques described in this chapter will help you persuade others to get support for your proposed initiatives, especially when they affect other parts of the company. The knowledge you display about how the organization works and your record of delivering on commitments also contribute to your impact in the eyes of senior executives. Your ability to project executive presence, the topic of the next chapter, is another important part of the equation.

CHAPTER 8

FACTOR 6
Projecting Executive Presence

I f you think *executive presence* means "dress for success," personal grooming, and "looking like an executive," you'd be partially right—and, perhaps, fundamentally wrong. Of the six core selection factors that lie behind executive promotion decisions, executive presence is the most intuitive and most visceral. Often senior-level decision makers have difficulty pinning down exactly what executive presence is and claim that it's mostly a gut feeling on their part. While writing this book, I had a number of conversations with senior executives responsible for executive promotion and placement decisions in their companies. The vast majority agreed that executive presence was a requirement for someone to make it to the C-suite level. However, their definitions varied significantly, as did the indicators—what they looked for in determining a manager's level of executive presence.

A few of those I spoke with did talk about dress and how executives carry themselves. Dressing appropriately for the executive level is important to fitting in with other members of the senior management team, as well as representing the company well in interactions with external groups such as customers and community leaders. Most of those I spoke with, though, said that dress itself wasn't a big issue in their companies—unless the person's dress and grooming was somehow out of place and distracting. Everyone agreed, though, that the core of executive presence is displaying the self-confidence required to succeed at a higher level of leadership. In short, can the individual

- Take control of difficult, even unpredictable situations?
- Make tough decisions in a timely way?
- Engage constructively with other talented and strong-willed members of the executive team?

Although executive presence is tough to articulate, it's critical that you understand how senior-level decision makers define executive presence, why it's important, and what you need to do to display it. In the course of my work with executives and high-potential managers over the years, I've found that people with very different personalities and styles can project executive presence even though their personal packages—their dress, stature, and carriage—may vary significantly. To dive deeper into this vital yet sometimes elusive area, consider four managers—Jeremy Zimmer, Lydia Taylor, Frank Simmons, and Gene Hastings—who express executive presence in very different ways.

Jeremy Zimmer

Jeremy Zimmer, the head of a small business unit for a large, global financial services company, was an up-and-coming manager who was often described as "sent from central casting." He was well educated and had a record of success in a number of sales and marketing positions, including an international assignment in the company's European headquarters. Tall, athletic, and articulate, he captured people's attention when he walked into a room. His posture and body language conveyed an underlying sense of self-assurance. He often talked about putting on his "dress blues" (a well-fitted navy blue suit, red tie, and white shirt) for important customer meetings and presentations to the company's senior managers. His overall image was impressive.

Socially adept in virtually any setting, he was an excellent public speaker. Senior managers looked forward to his highly polished, informative, and persuasive presentations. He was especially effective in responding to questions—even challenging ones—that came up during his presentations. His responses to tough questions, even from very senior managers, were direct and well reasoned, and he never seemed to lose his poise. While professional and respectful in his interactions with senior executives, there was never a sense that he felt anxious or cowed.

Jeremy was an assertive, take-charge manager who signaled that he expected to be listened to. He was described as results oriented and someone who held people accountable for delivering on their commitments. Although invariably ethical, he was a tough taskmaster. His people often said that working for Jeremy was not for the faint of heart. They knew in no uncertain terms if he was displeased with their performance. Still, his people performed for him, and members of the company's senior management team were impressed by his track record of results. There was no question that he was in line for future career advancement.

Lydia Taylor

If you entered a room filled with twenty managers, Lydia Taylor wouldn't immediately stand out—but that would change once the conversation started. A lawyer by training, she had joined her company, a large, well-known consumer products corporation based in the Midwest, in the legal department several years ago. In addition to excellent legal training, she possessed strong people skills and organizational ability. Since coming to work for the company, she had shown a real interest in learning the business and enjoyed working with business leaders, who applauded her ability to talk in simple business terms instead of legalese. Not only did her legal expertise make her highly credible within the legal department, she also seemed to have the rare ability to effectively manage highly skilled and highly independent staff. She had accompanied the company's general counsel on a number of visits to outside regulatory bodies. Each time the feedback the general counsel received about Lydia from the outside groups had been very positive.

Lydia tended to be soft spoken, and her dress and hair style, although tasteful and professional, would hardly be called flashy. It was in meetings, especially when she worked with senior managers on complex business and legal issues, that her presence as a leader shone through. She wasn't a dominant, table-pounding type. Rather, she was a superb listener and had an unerring sense of timing. She never barged into the conversation at the wrong time or competed with others for airtime. She seemed to find exactly the right time to make her point in a straightforward, unrushed way. Described by others as unflappable, she maintained her calm, composed demeanor even when others got emotional. She used her dry sense of humor to defuse tension in meetings and was able to find the right time and the right words to guide the group's conversation where she wanted it to go. When challenged by others, she stood her ground in a nonconfrontational way, but she made it clear that she expected her points to be considered and responded to.

Overall, her style suggested a collaborative approach to solving business problems. However, if she felt that an issue, whether legal or related to the business, was central to success or represented a vulnerability to the corporation, she would pursue it until it was addressed to her satisfaction. Over time she developed a reputation within the company for competence, people management skills, and the ability to balance her role as a resource to the business with taking a strong stand when she felt the company's interests were at stake. She was also well respected by external groups, including the regulatory bodies that were important to the company's success. As a result, senior management saw her as a strong candidate to become general counsel when the time was right.

Frank Simmons

I first learned about Frank Simmons when his company, a large manufacturing firm, asked me to lead a series of succession planning discussions with a group of its senior executives. The team had come together to review a number of candidates for executive-level positions, including Frank, a long-time employee who was director of manufacturing operations. It was clear that Frank was highly respected personally and professionally. "The heart and soul of the company," claimed one of the senior executives, a sentiment that was roundly echoed by the others participating in the discussion.

In the course of its conversation, the group identified Frank's major strengths and development needs as a leader.

Among the strengths were knowledge of the business, financial skills, the ability to create and monitor plans to achieve results, high performance standards, the ability to improve performance year over year, and the ability to create and manage a highly productive team. When we discussed his limitations, nothing truly significant emerged. Although he was described as a student of the industry, the executives felt he could stretch his strategic thinking further. He was described as a bit rough around the edges, especially in his dealings with customers and suppliers. None of these, however, were seen as serious deficiencies.

Nevertheless, for all of his experience and leadership skills, there was a noticeable lack of enthusiasm as the executives spoke about Frank—a lack of enthusiasm I was quick to probe. At first the group was quiet. Then one executive spoke up: "Frank's a tremendous asset to the company. I just can't see him at our level dealing with the kinds of issues we face." Although that one comment captured the feeling of the group, the executives around the table confessed that they couldn't quite put their finger on exactly what led them to that conclusion. Given the fact that the group was having trouble describing what Frank lacked, the conversation about him soon ended with the conclusion that he was at the right level within the company.

After that meeting ended, I had a chance to connect individually with several of the executives who had been part of the group to get more insight into Frank. Here's the portrait that emerged. Everyone had the utmost respect, even affection, for Frank, a manager who was highly valued for his commitment and contribution to the company. Several aspects of his personal style, however, tended to come up repeatedly. Although a good-looking guy, Frank tended to be a little rumpled in his dress, and his posture was a bit hunched.

Over the years he had made a number of presentations to the members of the company's executive team. His presentations were always solid and well prepared. However, it was clear that he was not entirely comfortable speaking to that group, and his body language telegraphed his discomfort. Although he knew virtually every member of the executive team well, he looked nervous. He tended to shuffle, and his hand and arm gestures seemed timid and constrained. When members of the executive team questioned or challenged him, he seemed to be thrown off-balance, and his responses were often somewhat rambling and long-winded. Some executives complained that he gave much more information than was necessary to respond to their questions.

On occasion, strong, heated debate about an issue broke out among members of the team during Frank's presentations. At such times, he seemed hesitant to insert himself into the conversation. In these senior management settings, he came across as overly deferential to the executives present and unable to get his points across with conviction—even when he had thoroughly researched the issue at hand. This led to questions about whether Frank could hold his own in discussions at the executive level.

In the course of these conversations with the senior executives, I asked people to explain why Frank didn't shine in his interactions with customers and suppliers. Their comments pointed to several issues. Frank was described as laid back and didn't come off as sufficiently professional. Although he listened politely to the issues and concerns expressed by customers, his responses were on occasion vague and noncommittal. That, combined with his rumpled dress, raised question marks about his ability to represent the company and build credibility with outside groups that were important to the company's success.

Gene Hastings

Gene Hastings joined his firm, a large engineering company, as an entry-level project engineer right out of college. Technically skilled and affable, he had risen to the level of senior project engineer. If you spent time with Gene, it was hard not to like and respect him. He knew the business, worked hard, had great values, and had shown the ability over the years to complete the most difficult and complex projects on time and on budget. He was viewed as a future leader by several of the company's executives.

Given Gene's perceived potential, the company arranged for me to work with him as a coach. When I met him, we talked at length about his career background and his goals for the future. These included leading one of the company's major operating divisions. It was clear to me that he took his work as a leader seriously and was genuinely concerned about the well-being of his people—but that he might well devote some time to tidying his office given the piles of folders strewn on the floor. He expressed real enthusiasm about the coaching I could provide him. As is often the case when I kick off a coaching assignment, I suggested to Gene that he complete an online 360-degree feedback survey, and we also agreed on a list of people for me to interview.

When I received the results of Gene's survey, it confirmed the same set of strengths that emerged from the interviews. He was an extremely well-rounded manager, precisely the reason the company wanted to invest in his career development. He was an accomplished project manager who knew how to rally the people who worked with him to meet customer needs and ensure that projects were completed on time. In addition to his engineering skills, he was well versed in managing the financials of large construction projects and was able to meet project profitability targets even under trying circumstances. People across the company genuinely liked working with Gene. In such a technically oriented company, his engineering background, knowledge of the business, project management expertise, and leadership ability combined to make him a strong candidate for future advancement.

But as is frequently the case, the interviews hinted at some important development issues that fell under the heading of executive presence. Although people at all levels went out of their way to sing Gene's praises, I heard recurrent comments about his organizational skills. At first, I was somewhat confused since I had been told that Gene and his team had a record of delivering on major project commitments on a consistent basis. As I continued to probe during the interviews, several important issues came to the surface.

Although Gene worked extremely hard and was able to follow up on a whole host of details on highly complex projects, people described him as harried, rushed, frazzled, and disorganized. When I asked for examples, I heard that Gene was late to meetings more often than not and that people often saw him racing down the hallway as he flew from one meeting to another. When he arrived, his papers and files were often askew, and it seemed to take him several minutes to settle down, switch gears, and get into the flow of the meeting. A number of people commented on the clutter in his office, wondering how he could find anything—let alone remember who on his team was responsible for what. As one person said, "I think the world of Gene, but there's a sense that events are driving him instead of the other way around."

After completing the interviews, I made a point of connecting with Gene's boss to discuss what I had picked up.

I asked his manager if he had shared this feedback with Gene. Somewhat sheepishly, he confessed that although he had hinted at Gene's personal organizational problems on a couple of occasions, he had not fully leveled with him knowing the pressure he was under. Besides he had never viewed these issues as major barriers until my feedback helped him see more clearly the link between Gene's apparent disorganization and his chances of operating successfully at the executive level. "If he's so poorly organized and seemingly overwhelmed at his current level, how could he possibly handle more responsibility?" his boss asked with rising concern.

When I met with Gene, I laid out the feedback as clearly and objectively as I could. As we got to the issue of executive presence, his initial response, not surprisingly, was somewhat defensive. But as we talked, and as I had expected, he started to internalize the feedback, allowing us to discuss ways he could respond to it.

Over the next six months, Gene showed he could deal with feedback—even feedback that went to the heart of his personal and leadership style. When, as part of the coaching, I conducted a series of follow-up interviews several months later, I heard Gene described in some new terms: relaxed, under control, buttoned up, and leader-like. Clearly he had worked to accomplish this result, and what he did during that period of time is telling.

Gene started with some pretty basic things related to personal organization and time management. He spent

most of a weekend organizing his office and met with
a senior executive's assistant to get ideas about creating a better filing system. He began to schedule time to
prepare for major meetings and made sure his materials for
each meeting were organized in advance. He set a goal of
arriving at major meetings a few minutes in advance of the
meeting's start time. This allowed him to engage in small
talk with the other attendees before the meeting started.
More important, it helped him switch gears from the topic
of the previous meeting so he could begin to focus on the
agenda of the new meeting. He also tried to become more
alert to his emotional blood pressure and the image he was
projecting to others. In reality, there were days when he
was scrambling to stay on top of things, and his days were
often packed with one meeting after the other. Nevertheless, he tried to remain conscious of the need to walk down
the hall at a controlled, professional pace.

As he thought about the times when he felt overwhelmed keeping track of a myriad of project details, he
began to realize that he was taking on too much responsibility and not demanding enough of his direct reports.
He began to delegate some follow-up responsibilities to
his staff members. A few things fell through the cracks initially, but as his direct reports became aware of what he
expected of them, most rose to the challenge.

All of these changes required a lot of hard work on
Gene's part. However, the company's senior executives
began to view him in a different light. He and his team

continued to produce strong results, and he got great feedback from his customers about the quality of his work. Now the senior executives began to sense greater capability on Gene's part and felt renewed confidence in his ability to succeed at the executive level. As a result, Gene's boss began looking for new assignments that would broaden him beyond his base of project management experience—with an eye toward Gene's playing a bigger role in the future.

THE ELEMENTS OF EXECUTIVE PRESENCE

Virtually all of us would agree that executive presence—the ability to look and sound like a leader—is a requirement for advancement to the executive level. But senior-level decision makers often struggle to describe why a manager does or doesn't have executive presence. That by itself creates an obstacle to you in taking steps to improve your presence as a leader. However, although it may be based on gut feel, it's important to know what's going on when more senior managers observe you and draw conclusions about your style and presence as a potential executive.

At its most basic level, executive presence is the external and visible manifestation of your ability to succeed at the executive level. If successfully displayed, your executive presence indicates that you can

- Maintain your composure and clarity of thought under stress and pressure.

- Take control of difficult-to-manage situations—as opposed to being passive or overwhelmed by a crisis.

- Make tough, often unpopular decisions without procrastinating.

- Quickly build confidence on the part of others so they will follow your lead.

- Project a sense of optimism that difficult challenges can be overcome.

- Be taken seriously as a member of the executive team: being able to hold your own in spirited discussions with other smart, talented, and opinionated executives and persuading others to adopt your point of view.

- Take a minority position on an issue you think is critical to the company's success and hold your ground when challenged.

- Represent the company well with external groups: customers, suppliers, community groups, the media, regulators, governmental bodies, and industry groups.

Executive presence is a sort of preview of coming attractions. Your ability to project executive presence builds confidence that you'll be able to handle the kinds of challenges executives are forced to deal with at the C-suite level.

Executive presence takes different forms in different people. Jeremy Zimmer exhibited a classic, traditional style in his interactions with others. However, as executive ranks in many companies have become increasingly more diverse, executive presence can be displayed effectively in a variety of ways. Nonetheless, several underlying elements collectively contribute to the ability to project executive presence. These elements flow from your self-confidence and sense of being in control of yourself and events around you.

The Impact of Dress and Physical Carriage

Executive presence is clearly something much more fundamental than dress, grooming, and carriage, that is, how you carry yourself physically. But they are all part of the total equation that add up to executive presence. As a starting point, several rules of thumb are useful in thinking about dress and grooming. It's often said that you should dress for the level you'd like to achieve—or at least one level above where you are currently.

Look around and see how executives in your company dress. In some companies, you'll see expensive suits, snappy ties, and designer outfits. In other companies, the emphasis is on tasteful but more conservative dress. Whether it's your clothes, your hair style, or your jewelry, it's important not to wear anything that, in your company's environment, will distract people and cause them not to take you seriously as a professional. For example, I've heard otherwise talented managers described as dressing like a "used-car salesman" or a "schoolmarm." The connotations are not flattering—nor are they insignificant. People tend not to trust a used-car salesman, and schoolmarms are not typically thought of as creative and risk taking, two qualities central to innovation and change.

If you have any question about how you are viewed in terms of dress, grooming, or personal carriage, try to find a buddy, ideally someone within your company who is familiar with the environment. Ask this person to give you the straight scoop about your appearance, along with recommendations about things you might change. Keep in mind that most bosses (who are hesitant to give feedback about subjective things) tend to be uncomfortable with issues such as dress and grooming. Unfortunately I've observed that this is especially true with male bosses of women and people of color. So if you can find a peer or an executive in another part of the company who will level with you about any aspects of your appearance that are getting in the way, that person is truly worth his or her weight in gold.

Public Speaking: A Moment of Truth

After reading the descriptions of Jeremy Zimmer, Lydia Taylor, and Frank Simmons, you may be somewhat surprised by the premium that organizations place on the ability to speak in public, especially in situations when senior managers are in the audience. Keep in mind that the ability to speak effectively and persuasively to groups is related to two of the core selection factors: communicating your strategic vision and building support for innovation and change. But there are other matters involved when you speak to groups, and in many companies, they make your presentations an important moment of truth.

By definition, you are highly visible when you make a presentation to a group, and in many companies, formal presentations are often the setting in which managers are most likely to come in contact with senior executives to discuss business issues. Most people admit to some level of anxiety when speaking in public, so how you handle yourself while making a presentation is often viewed as an indication of how you deal with pressure and stress. Your body language, tone of voice, and how quick on your feet you are in responding to questions become in effect a proxy for how you would respond to stressful situations at the executive level.

Note how Frank Simmons's executive presence is undermined by his obvious nervousness when he presents to his company's senior management team. His body language, his shuffling feet, and constrained gestures signal his discomfort, and his verbal style in response to questions becomes long-winded and even rambling. To the extent that you, like Simmons, come off as nervous and uncomfortable in presentation situations, this is more than a simple communication problem. It may cause senior-level decision makers to question your drive to lead, especially your ability to make difficult, often unpopular decisions under pressure. Recall that this is one of the nonnegotiable factors highlighted in Chapter One.

It's not necessary to be a spell-binding speaker to be successful as an executive, although your presentation skills become more important the higher up you go. However, it's a good investment of your time and money to take public speaking classes or work with a communications coach with the goal of becoming a poised and capable speaker. Focus on developing a communication style that is direct and concise in conveying your points. Get feedback on your body language (your posture, hand and arm gestures, how you stand in front of a group, even your walk) so that it projects the level of self-confidence and conviction in expressing your opinions expected of an executive.

In your training, pay particular attention to techniques for handling the question-and-answer portion of your presentation. This is an excellent opportunity for you to display your ability to maintain your poise when challenged and think on your feet. You may interpret a question from a senior executive as a sign that she disagrees with your argument or position. In many cases, however, the executive's question may simply be a request for more information. In others, it may be an attempt to test your ability to respond on the spot. Take a moment to make sure you understand the executive's question fully, and consider what the executive is looking for in a response. Try to answer as directly as you can, and avoid the temptation to give more information than is needed. If the executive who asked the question wants more information, she'll usually ask a follow-up question to probe the issue further.

Of course, there will be occasions when an executive attending one of your presentations expresses disagreement with some portion of your presentation, a situation that calls for a special level of poise. Note that Frank Simmons seemed to lose his composure in such situations and tended to become overly deferential to the senior executives present—to the point of backtracking on a well-researched position. By contrast, Jeremy Zimmer, while certainly professional and respectful of the rank of more senior executives attending his presentations, was poised in responding to their questions and able to express his positions with a sense of conviction. In the process, he demonstrated his ability to take and maintain a position on something he felt was important for the business—and that augured well for his ability to do so as an executive.

In addition to investing in formal presentation training and coaching, take advantage of every chance you get to hone your public speaking skills. Interestingly, although most people admit to being anxious about speaking in public, presentation ability is the skill that is easiest for most managers to develop. It does take work and practice. However, many managers are pleasantly surprised to see how increased polish and self-confidence in public speaking settings often translate into greater poise and self-assurance in other situations. Examples include how they walk into a room, how they articulate their points in a meeting, and the professionalism they project in interactions with important customers or government officials.

FINDING YOUR VOICE

As you attempt to strengthen and project your executive presence to others, keep in mind that this is an area where there is no one size fits all. How Lydia Taylor conveyed executive presence was very different from how Jeremy Zimmer did it, but she was highly effective nonetheless. Writers talk about someone finding their voice, one's unique and distinctive style, and it's a useful concept to keep in mind when you think about executive presence. Not everyone is cut out to be a Jeremy Zimmer—either physically or in terms of his commanding type A personality. Trying to adopt a style that's not consistent with your personality is a losing proposition. You'll come off as artificial and unconvincing.

Instead identify your assets, and leverage them to the hilt in order to project your self-confidence and sense of being in control. For Lydia Taylor, it was her listening ability, sense of humor, sense of timing, and ability to remain objective when others got emotional—all qualities she employed to move groups in the direction she sought. Not a driver of others in a traditional sense, she was patient and persistent, but she didn't let herself get run over by others who were more assertive. As a result, in her somewhat understated way, she was successful in building confidence on the part of her company's senior managers that she could play at the executive level, including representing the company well in interactions with important external groups such as regulatory bodies, outside counsel, and industry associations.

As you try to identify your voice, how you'll project your executive presence to others, keep in mind two constant elements of a successful executive style: the ability to convey a sense of optimism to others and a sense of being in control of yourself and those around you. In any organization there will be naysayers who are quick to point out the problems and why some new idea won't work. As one retired senior executive told me, although wearing rose-colored glasses is not desirable, neither is a tone of gloom, doom, and negativity. Especially if you're an analytical type who can quickly spot the potential pitfalls in any course of action, consider the tone you project to others. Rather than becoming mired in why something can't be done, a leader sees possibilities and can lead people to overcome obstacles.

In developing your executive presence, be mindful of seemingly small things that can trip you up and undermine the image you are trying to project. For example, remember some of the terms initially used to describe Gene Hastings: *rushed, harried,* and *scrambling to stay on top of things.* These descriptions raised red flags in the minds of his company's senior managers when they tried to envision him operating at the executive level.

Some managers are more buttoned up in their leadership style than others. However, projecting to others that you are disorganized and harried raises concerns on the part of senior-level decision makers—even if you are ultimately able to deliver on your responsibilities in a high-quality way. Think about how others in your company see you as you walk through the halls or arrive at a meeting. Do you usually arrive at meetings on time and in a relaxed and seemingly well-prepared manner—or are you typically a few minutes late and harried? Do you project to others a sense of being distracted and having trouble keeping up with all of the responsibilities on your plate?

Such apparent disorganization can hurt you in several ways. Executives are responsible for coordinating numerous activities and typically manage large staffs. As a result, they need to project a sense that they are in control. To the extent that senior-level decision makers perceive that you are struggling to manage at your current level, they will be leery of giving you more responsibility.

One important element of executive presence is projecting a sense of composure and self-control—even when the pot is boiling over and you're being hit with a number of unforeseen events. Executives are a bit like the proverbial duck: calm and collected above the water line—and paddling like mad below it. Successful executives are masters of switching gears: transitioning their focus—intellectually and emotionally—from one topic to another. If this tends to be hard for you to do, try to identify the techniques that help you ease the transition as you move from one topic or meeting to another during the course of the workday. For some, it's a casual conversation with peers. For others, a five-minute break in the action clears their mind.

Sometimes this involves pretty basic techniques in time management and personal organization. However, none of this is easy. Productivity improvement efforts have increased workloads for virtually everyone in most organizations. Fewer and fewer managers have assistants, so you're typically called on to do more administrative work yourself. E-mail and advances in telecommunications have extended the workday for almost every manager. That said, your challenge remains the same as it always has been: to project to others the sense that you are in control of the people and events around you and have unused capacity to take on more responsibility.

EXECUTIVE PRESENCE: A PRACTICED ART

When you observe a senior executive who exudes self-confidence and presence, it usually looks entirely natural. However, that doesn't mean that executive presence is achieved without preparation. More often, what comes across as effortless and a natural extension of an executive's personality is actually the result of painstaking practice. Most executives I know rehearse for major presentations. One drives his family crazy by doing repeated dry runs in the bathroom shower. As a result, when he speaks, he is able to focus his attention on his audience—how they are responding and what they seem interested in hearing—as opposed to what he's going to say. Another executive makes notes before leaving a voice message for senior executives at her company. She wants to make sure that her message is succinct and well articulated and delivered in the persuasive, self-confident tone of voice one expects of an executive. Most executives are also extremely careful about the quality of their written work—both quick e-mails as well as more formal reports and memos. They realize that poor spelling or grammar or, in the case of e-mails, a hasty, emotional response can undermine the sense of self-control and professionalism they want to convey.

Projecting executive presence is not totally natural to most of us. Instead it starts with a good understanding of the roots of executive presence and how to breed confidence on the part of the senior executives who make promotional decisions in your organization. So focus your developmental efforts on displaying the building blocks that add up to a commanding presence—the self-confidence, composure, positive assertiveness, attitude of optimism, and sense of being in control—in a way that's consistent with your style and personality.

CHAPTER 9

Career Development Strategies

C hapters Three through Eight probed deeply into the six core factors that are vital for promotion to the executive level in most companies. Certainly there are things you can do in most jobs to develop your abilities relating to these six areas. However, several of the factors require a broad range of job experiences to fully develop the necessary skills. Think back through the core selection factors. Top-notch strategic thinking demands a breadth of perspective on the business and the industry. To successfully manage large-scale change or work effectively with others across organizational boundaries, you need a deep understanding of how the organization works and how a decision in one part of the organization affects other parts of the company. It's extremely difficult to develop the breadth of perspective and organizational knowledge required of an executive if your career has been spent exclusively in one part of the company.

Most managers who aspire to the executive level understand the benefits of a broad base of job experience. However, they frequently run into roadblocks when they try to move to new job assignments in another part of the organization. Regardless of how much they may espouse the benefits of so-called stretch assignments for their future leaders, many companies lack the mechanisms required to enable such job moves. In most organizations you'll need to take the initiative in managing your career to overcome these obstacles. In this chapter, I discuss seven career development strategies designed to put yourself in a position to develop and display the six core selection skills:

1. Increasing your visibility within the company

2. Building your external network

3. Considering a lateral move

4. Engineering a development assignment

5. Demonstrating your learning ability

6. Identifying the right stretch assignment

7. Finding creative ways to develop in your current job

Each of these strategies is designed to promote the range of experiences you need to accomplish your career goals and advance to the executive level.

INCREASING YOUR VISIBILITY WITHIN THE COMPANY

"Don't hide your light under a bushel" is a saying in the Bible that applies to managers who seek to be promoted to the executive level. Enhancing your visibility to senior leaders across the organization is an important part of getting on your company's list for career advancement. As your reputation as an up-and-coming leader becomes known to a greater number of executives, more development opportunities are likely to come your way.

Some years back I had a chance to observe Eileen Drake's meteoric rise within her company. An M.B.A. by background, she was a finance manager in one of the company's business units and was well liked and well regarded by those in her group. However, hers was a relatively slow-moving company that wasn't always equipped to spot potential stars, even those like Eileen who had been with the company for a number of years.

Based on her analytical skills and knowledge of the business, Eileen was chosen to serve on an important task force during a time when the company was planning a large-scale change in its business processes. Ed, the leader of Eileen's task force, was an executive from a different part of the company. As task force leader, he also sat on the overall project steering committee composed of executives from across the company.

Eileen recognized that her work on the task force represented an opportunity to learn more about the company and spread her wings beyond the business unit where she had worked since joining the company. Ed was extremely impressed by Eileen's contribution to the group. At project steering committee meetings, other company executives began to hear Ed sing Eileen's praises. He spoke about her drive and commitment, her analytical skills, and her ability to work with other members of the task force.

When her task force assignment was completed, Eileen's career began to take off. After working in relative obscurity within the company for a number of years, she was promoted three times in the next five years. Along the way she moved from finance to product development and was ultimately named general manager of a medium-sized business unit. Eileen was immensely talented, but it was her work on Ed's task force—and the glowing endorsements he gave other senior executives—that lit the fuse for her rapid career growth.

Eileen Drake's experience illustrates the power of organizational buzz. That's when executives across the company begin talking about a promising manager, causing her career stock to rise. As you manage your career, look for opportunities to participate in cross-functional projects that can increase your exposure to more senior executives who can create that buzz. Make sure your manager knows of your interest so he can recommend you when such initiatives are being staffed. These kinds of opportunities abound in most companies, if you are alert to them.

Examples include participating on a major company task force like the one Eileen served on, helping to organize a major customer's visit to company headquarters, or joining a team charged with researching industry best practices and presenting the results to senior executives.

Such opportunities to increase your visibility are only that: potential chances to shine. As you look for ways to increase your exposure to more senior executives, keep working to develop the leadership skills that relate to the six core selection factors. That way, when an opportunity presents itself, you'll be prepared to rise to the challenge and showcase your abilities.

BUILDING YOUR EXTERNAL NETWORK

Over the years I have seen extremely hard-working and committed managers commit a major misstep in managing their careers. These managers become inwardly focused, that is, preoccupied with events inside their own company. As a result, they miss opportunities to develop their network outside the organization. This is a trap that's all too common—and one I encourage you to avoid.

It's easy to get caught up in activities within your company—including getting sucked into the company rumor mill. However, developing an inward focus has a number of downsides in terms of your future career success. Whether you're in a market-facing role like sales, marketing, or general management or in an internal role like information technology or human resources, the keys to your strategic and innovative thinking are much more likely to lie outside the company than within it. Managers who focus their attention primarily on internal company activities tend to cut themselves off from customers, marketplace trends, new industry practices, and the diverse sources of information required to jump-start their creative thinking. In addition, your lack of external relationships serves as an obstacle when it comes time to explore jobs outside the company.

If such an inward focus describes you, start by committing yourself to developing your external network. Industry groups and professional associations are a good place to begin. They provide excellent opportunities to practice and develop your leadership skills as you build relationships outside the company. At meetings of such groups, you'll have a chance to hear different perspectives about trends in your own and other industries and learn about best practice approaches that may be applicable to your company. Your external network can also provide invaluable insight into job opportunities outside your company if and when you decide to test the outside market.

CONSIDERING A LATERAL MOVE

As you think about future job assignments that can contribute to your career advancement, remember that a promotion to the next level may not always be the best route to long-term success. Over the years I've seen highly talented people progress straight up the silo of their discipline, whether it's finance or marketing. In the process, they develop marvelous functional skills. However, due to their narrow view of the business, many encounter obstacles later when they try to advance to more senior positions. To avoid this fate, consider the benefits of a lateral move—an assignment at the same level as your current position that could broaden your perspective, strengthen your leadership skills, and create a foundation for long-term career success. Carol Bartz, CEO of Yahoo! recently said, "You need to build your careers not as a ladder, but as a pyramid. You need to have a base of experience because it's a much more stable structure. . . . That involves taking lateral moves. And it involves getting out of your comfort zone."[1]

The experience you gain from the right lateral move can provide new insights into how your company works. Under the right set of circumstances, moving into a role that is a departure from your prior career experience will pay big dividends in your ability to lead others. Typically the higher up an executive goes, the less she is able to rely on her own expertise and the more she needs to leverage her ability to manage and motivate others. If a lateral move takes you away from your home base of experience, you'll be forced to rely on others and find new ways to add value.

From a career development standpoint, a lateral move to another function or unit within the company can be one of your best experiences—or your worst. So it's important to know the conditions that will maximize your chances of success. If you're a high-performing manager who knows how to get results, many executives in the company will want to have you on their team. Getting a new job therefore isn't the issue. What's important is negotiating a job move so it's part of an overall career plan. That helps you avoid getting sidetracked and stuck in an area of the organization that doesn't play to your strengths over the long haul. A job assignment that is part of a career development plan includes common understanding by all parties on three important points:

1. What you will learn and develop in the assignment

2. The support you'll get from your new boss and others to be successful

3. Where you can go in the organization if you succeed in the new job

Recognize that you are only negotiating a plan, not getting a promise. You still have to perform in the new assignment and demonstrate your ability to grow from the experience. But as Bartz suggests, the right lateral assignment—under the right set of circumstances—can provide a foundation of knowledge and experience that will stand you in good stead over the course of your career.

ENGINEERING A DEVELOPMENT ASSIGNMENT

A few, and only a few, of my clients have sophisticated succession planning and talent development programs. These companies devote considerable time to identifying potential future leaders and planning for their development. Bosses in these companies are expected to engage in career discussions with their best people and create tangible career plans. But again, we're talking about a distinct minority of organizations.

Most likely, jobs in your company are filled more by happenstance than by design and in response to short-term staffing needs rather than any long-term development goal. Often talented, upwardly aspiring managers are told to wait their turn for a promotion or a new developmental assignment. Worse, their career progress may be held back by a boss who is more than happy to see a top performer remain on his team to help meet his performance objectives.

If you find yourself in this latter kind of company, you'll need to take the initiative to move into the kinds of jobs that will help you prepare for the executive level. Engineering such assignments typically requires a fair amount of political astuteness and patience on your part. However, with skill and persistence, you can overcome many of the barriers that companies inadvertently put in the way of your career advancement.

Clearly, your ability to move into a new developmental assignment starts with top-notch performance in your current job. That makes you attractive to bosses in other parts of the organization. I also recommend that you review the nonnegotiables and deselection factors outlined in Chapter One that are part of the unwritten rules. An insensitive or abrasive style, a narrow or parochial perspective, question marks about your trustworthiness: any of these will reduce your marketability for new jobs in the company.

If your boss has not conducted a career discussion with you recently, I suggest you try to set up a time to meet. As you prepare to engage your boss in conversation about your career—especially new assignments that will help advance it—be mindful of the following:

- Your boss is probably not in a position to arrange a new assignment unilaterally.

- Her opinions about the options for future assignments may or may not represent the best advice for you.

- Assuming you are a good performer, your leaving the team would create a hole she'd have to fill.

So although your career discussions should begin with your boss, try to enlist her help in identifying other executives who can contribute to your career planning dialogue. Consistent with my advice in Chapter Two about seeking feedback from a number of executives, make sure your boss is in the loop with your career conversations with others.

Otherwise she'll fear you're out trying to arrange a new job with another executive and that she'll get left in the lurch.

Such career conversations—especially if they are spaced over a period of months so it doesn't seem as if you are simply lobbying for a new job—serve several purposes:

- The counsel you receive will help clarify your thinking about your career goals and alternative ways to achieve them.

- It gives your manager time to prepare to replace you when you move into a new assignment.

- You have a chance to build your relationships with executives across the company who can be instrumental to your career progress.

In the course of your conversations, it's extremely helpful if you can meet with your boss's boss. If your manager's boss is familiar with your career goals and the kinds of assignments you would find attractive, he's in a position to support you in moving to a new job. If he senses that your boss may be hesitant about your taking on a new assignment, he can also apply some positive pressure when the right assignment comes along. Finally, your boss and her manager can help you find ways to increase your visibility to executives in other parts of the organization. For example, I've seen one executive arrange for a manager to work on a project with members of another executive's staff with the express goal of greasing the skids for a future job move into that executive's organization.

One final caveat. In your career discussions, don't be surprised if executives and others, such as human resource managers who may get involved, are a bit vague about which future assignments are being targeted and a timetable for moving into them. For good reason, executives tend not to make specific promises about new developmental assignments since changes in business priorities or a resignation somewhere else in the organization can put a wrinkle in such development plans. Nonetheless, if you have orchestrated your career discussions carefully and shown the required amount of patience, you'll be pleased with the opportunities for career advancement that come your way.

DEMONSTRATING YOUR LEARNING ABILITY

In the past few years, it has become fashionable for succession planners and executives responsible for developing their companies' future leaders to speak about "learning ability." When most managers hear the term, they tend to think about someone's ability to take in new information or build new skills in a functional discipline—whether it's manufacturing, finance, or another field. That kind of learning is certainly important. However, it's useful to know how senior executives responsible for C-suite placements define *learning* and what they look for when a manager takes on a new developmental assignment.

In essence they are looking for what I call the learning gene. That gene has three main components:

1. Being a quick study: the ability to move up the learning curve rapidly when taking on a new situation or assignment, analyze situations quickly, and sort out the key issues in order to make good decisions

2. The ability to solicit feedback from others about how you're attacking problems, leading your organization, and interacting with others

3. Most important, the ability to fundamentally change your style and approach based on experience; that is, to learn from your successes and failures and modify your approach accordingly

The head of succession planning at one large, global corporation, for example, recently told me that senior executives there monitor managers closely when they move into a new developmental assignment. In evaluating a manager, they look for several things: the manager's ability to master the assignment quickly, produce results even if the new role is a departure from his or her prior experience, and adapt to a new level of complexity without getting overwhelmed.

Advancing your career through a series of new job assignments is like playing pinball: each time you win, you get to play again. So as you progress in your career, view every new assignment you take on as a chance to develop new skills and demonstrate your ability to learn and adapt. Be mindful of the fact that in many companies, the learning ability you display in taking on a new assignment is viewed as an important leading indicator of your chances of success in higher-level positions in the future. As a result, make sure your ability to learn from an assignment is clearly visible to others.

IDENTIFYING THE RIGHT STRETCH ASSIGNMENT

In the course of my assessment and coaching work, I often have a chance to talk with executives about their careers, especially the experiences they've had along the way that were most useful in getting them to where they are. You'd expect them to talk about big promotions and big successes. But those aren't the experiences they usually highlight. Rather, they tend to talk about new job assignments that challenged them in unexpected ways and helped them grow in the process.

The specific jobs they describe vary widely. However, their assignments have some common characteristics:

- The manager wasn't fully prepared for the position and had to develop new skills and perspectives quickly.

- The position was outside the manager's area of expertise, causing her to learn to rely on others.

- The manager was responsible for producing results from day 1 in the job.

As you think about new job assignments that would accelerate your career progress, keep in mind the six core selection factors used in making C-suite-level placement decisions. Then look for jobs that will help you expand your perspective on the business and industry, broaden your network of relationships within and outside the organization, and deepen your knowledge of how the company operates.

Over the past few years, I've had a chance to work with several managers—Paul Fairweather, Roberta Whiting, Jack Phillips, and Bob Hendricks—whose stories might stimulate your thinking about new assignments that could be highly developmental for you.

Paul Fairweather

Paul Fairweather, a southerner by background, was a promising young engineer who worked for a global consumer products corporation based in the United States. A few years after joining the company, he came home from work one day with his head reeling. His boss had just asked him to take a new position as manager of a small manufacturing facility based in Asia. This was a huge step for a young man who had never been more than five hundred miles from home. As head of the manufacturing facility, he would be responsible for a staff of sixty—a big jump from his current team of five.

Years later, when I spoke with Paul, he was the head of one of the company's largest operating groups. He credited much of his success to that Asian assignment. Beyond global perspective, he had learned how to delegate and manage a large group. "Otherwise," he laughed, "I would have been sunk before I got started." He also gained confidence in his judgment since the job threw so many decisions at him on a daily basis—at a time when he was thousands of miles away from all of the support resources a manager located at a corporate headquarters is able to access.

Roberta Whiting

Roberta Whiting had risen from part-time stock clerk during college to district manager of a large, fast-growing retailer. As district manager, she was responsible for ten large stores in a two-state area. Reflecting on where she was at that point in her career, Roberta said her work was all about driving weekly sales, and she knew her marketplace inside out. It was a real feather in her cap when she was invited to take a new job in the company's retail strategy and planning department in the company's headquarters.

When I spoke with Roberta some years later, she described her first months in her new job as both disorienting and exhilarating. For the first time in years, she didn't have a staff to manage, and she wasn't responsible for sales or store profit. Instead she had time to think about retail expansion strategies and sales programs that could boost sales across the entire company. In the past, she had often wondered what corporate staff people did every day and secretly questioned whether they were worth the expense of their salaries. In her new corporate staff job, she was able to develop a broad network across all of the retail districts and most of the corporate departments as well. When it came time to recommend a new sales program, she realized there were a lot of people in a variety of functions she needed to convince about the merits of her plan.

Later in her career, Roberta became head of all of the company's retail stores and led a huge organization. Although she had spent only two years in the retail strategy and planning role, she claimed that the experience had made a world of difference in her ability to marshal company resources to drive sales. Time and again, she relied on her knowledge of the corporate organization, especially the roles and objectives of the various units, to influence and persuade other executives to get the support her store's division needed to succeed.

Jack Phillips

An M.B.A. by training, Jack Phillips had started with his company, a large energy corporation, in its finance development program. He and the other program members had been hired from top schools and were viewed as the crack troops of the company's finance organization. After several years honing his skills in a series of corporate finance jobs, Jack was asked to become finance manager for an operating group located in the field away from company headquarters. In his new role, Jack loved being able to participate in business decisions with the other members of the unit's management team. As the president of the group said at the time, "Jack gets the business. He doesn't want to simply keep track of the numbers. He wants to help us find ways to grow."

Jack was so well regarded by the members of the group's management team that he was asked to take over as general manager of a small business unit. This was a highly unusual move for a finance manager, and he jumped at the chance. For the next three years, Jack was responsible for his unit's profit-and-loss statement. His team included sales, marketing, operations, and human resource staff. As he said years later, "It was so different from anything else I'd ever done." Instead of analyzing results and preparing financial projections, he had to make decisions on a wide range of issues, often at a dizzying pace.

As much as he enjoyed the assignment, Jack decided he would be most successful in a finance position over the long term. Ultimately he became chief financial officer for the entire corporation. One of the reasons he got the top finance job was his reputation as an executive committed to the success of the company's operating groups. From his days as a general manager, he understood that business unit leaders are on the firing line to respond to customer demands and make difficult trade-off decisions to ensure both short-term and long-term success. Without a doubt, he understood the importance of budgeting and financial control in running a big corporation. However, he also wanted to make sure that all finance staff throughout the company contributed to the success of the business, an attitude that made him stand out from other finance leaders.

Bob Hendricks

Bob Hendricks was a hard-charging and highly successful sales manager for a large printing supplies company. Early in his career, he'd been given responsibility for a sales district in an area near the company's headquarters. Creative and results oriented, he knew how to motivate aggressive, self-motivated salespeople like himself.

Bob had caught the eye of the company's senior vice president of sales (SVP). His sales district was an important one for the company, so the SVP didn't want to move Bob out of that position. However, the SVP was looking for ways to expand Bob's responsibilities and help him grow in the process. About that time, the head of the company's call center decided to retire. That provided the SVP with the opportunity he was looking for. While still retaining responsibility for his sales district, Bob was asked to take over as manager of the call center and its staff of one hundred.

Some years later Bob told me he had assumed his new role with some trepidation. He knew how to build a sales organization and get the best out of salespeople.

197

The call center was completely different. The work of call center representatives was tightly controlled—as opposed to his salespeople, who operated quite independently. Managers in the call center spent a considerable amount of time measuring the representatives' work and trying to tweak work processes to find productivity gains. In addition, Bob quickly came to understand that team interaction and group morale were important to call center performance, and he spent time participating in a variety of staff events.

Over the years, Bob rose to become head of sales and marketing for the company. Of all his positions along the way, his responsibility for the call center was one of the most useful he'd had. It was there, he told me, that he had learned to manage staff very different from himself and the field salespeople he knew well. He realized that different kinds of people were motivated by different things, and he learned to flex his communication style and management approach to reflect the needs of the group. These new skills stood him in good stead when he became responsible for a large organization comprising a number of departments, each staffed with different kinds of people.

■ ■

These stories of successful executives contain some important lessons. As you plot your career future, don't become overly focused on the next rung on your company's ladder. Instead seek out assignments that will stretch you in new ways. Depending on the nature of the company's business, it could be an international assignment to broaden your horizons. It could be setting up a joint venture or strategic alliance with another company—something that will increase your external perspective and help develop your skills in influence and persuasion. Or it could be leading a start-up organization where you'll need to show your resourcefulness and ability to make decisions outside your area of expertise. Years in the future—like Paul, Roberta, Jack, and Bob—these may be the assignments you point to as being the most pivotal in achieving career success.

FINDING CREATIVE WAYS TO DEVELOP IN YOUR CURRENT ASSIGNMENT

Although stretch assignments form the backbone of career development for most executives, there are undoubtably ways you can build new skills in your current job. I've already highlighted the benefits of serving on high-profile tasks forces assembled to tackle projects that touch multiple parts of the company. For some managers, like Fred Henderson in Chapter Seven, executive coaching is extremely useful. In Fred's case, coaching provided him with the tools to build his working relationships with peers and expand his lateral management skills. I've also seen managers who gained from enrolling in an executive M.B.A. program. Although such programs require a great deal of time and commitment, they can expand your mental map of how the organization operates and help sharpen your strategic skills.

Less traditional opportunities for development in your current job abound in most organizations—if you are prepared to take the initiative and exercise some creativity. To find them, you'll need to look beyond conventional development approaches like classroom training to locate the people and experiences that can help orient you to new parts of the business and organization and build new skills. Four managers I've worked with—Fran Hopkins, Matt Jenkins, Tom Willoughby, and Stu Clement—illustrate the power of nontraditional development activities.

Fran Hopkins

Fran Hopkins had been targeted as an up-and-coming manager by her company, a global agricultural products corporation based in the Midwest. Fran had joined the company's R&D department after a number of years in academia. Combining book smarts with people smarts, she had shown the ability to organize the work of research scientists and manage their performance.

During the course of a project aimed at developing a new product for overseas export, Fran came into contact with the senior vice president of the company's international division. After several conversations, they devised a novel plan to increase Fran's exposure to the global marketplace. Over a ten-day period Fran accompanied the SVP on a tour of four of the company's South American subsidiaries. At each location, they visited company facilities and met with key customers. These market tours were scheduled to coincide with each subsidiary's annual business review. During these presentations, Fran heard the subsidiary general manager and the members of his team review business results, discuss competitive activity, and lay out strategies and plans for the coming year. After each review, she met with the international division's finance director to dig into the subsidiary's financial performance and budgets.

Fran later described this trip as her awakening to the diversity of the company's markets around the world. A few years later, she was able to put her new global perspective to work when she was promoted to an executive-level position responsible for a large R&D group that supported a number of international as well as domestic business units.

Matt Jenkins and Tom Willoughby

When I first met Matt Jenkins, he was a young finance manager for a large consumer products company. Early in his career, Matt had developed a relationship with Tom Willoughby, a well-regarded creative manager with the company. Independent of any corporately planned program, the two managers decided to tutor each other in their respective fields. For six months, they alternated training sessions. One week the finance manager, a graduate of a top business school, instructed the creative manager in financial analysis techniques and how to read financial statements. The next week the creative manager, a fine arts graduate who managed a staff of commercial artists, introduced the finance manager to the company's creative process.

Over the course of their careers, both were highly successful. Matt became a senior executive of a multibillion-dollar company that relied on its creative resources. When he retired, Tom was the executive responsible for leading one of the world's largest creative organizations. Each looks back to these home-grown tutorial sessions as having created a platform for career success. Matt gained insight into the creative process and how to motivate creative staff. Tom never lost his creative instincts, but he came away with a much deeper understanding of how the company made money—and what he learned about managing a budget stood him in good stead as the leader of a large organization.

Stu Clement

Some years ago I interviewed Stu Clement, a very senior corporate leader with a large energy company. In the course of the interview, I asked Stu about the developmental experiences he'd had in the course of his career.

To my surprise, he responded that one of his most beneficial experiences came when he volunteered to serve on the town board of the community where he had lived as a midlevel manager. He went on to explain that he had joined the company fresh out of business school and after a brief stint as a military officer. Early on with the company, he had quickly progressed through a series of management roles. As he did, he became used to giving staff members directives and having people jump to it based on his organizational rank and military bearing.

When he described his town board experience, Stu told me, somewhat tongue in cheek, "The other board members didn't know me from Adam and certainly didn't care that I was a rising executive with the company." Given the fact he had no organizational rank to rely on, he had to polish his skills in influence and persuasion to have an impact within the board.

As he progressed in his career, Stu became responsible for one of the company's largest business groups, a position in which he was required to deal with government officials and industry regulators. His organization included petroleum engineers, highly creative marketing staff, and facilities planning people. Some staff members responded to his directives without delay. Others needed to be persuaded to follow a course of action. According to Stu, what he learned about herding cats on the town board years before proved to be extremely valuable, especially when it came to working with government and industry officials who had no interest in being told what to do.

CRAFTING YOUR CAREER DEVELOPMENT PLAN

In essence these strategies, taken together, allow you to create and implement your plan for career development. Figure 9.1, the Constellation of Development Approaches, is a model I've used with many clients.

Figure 9.1 Constellation of Development Approaches

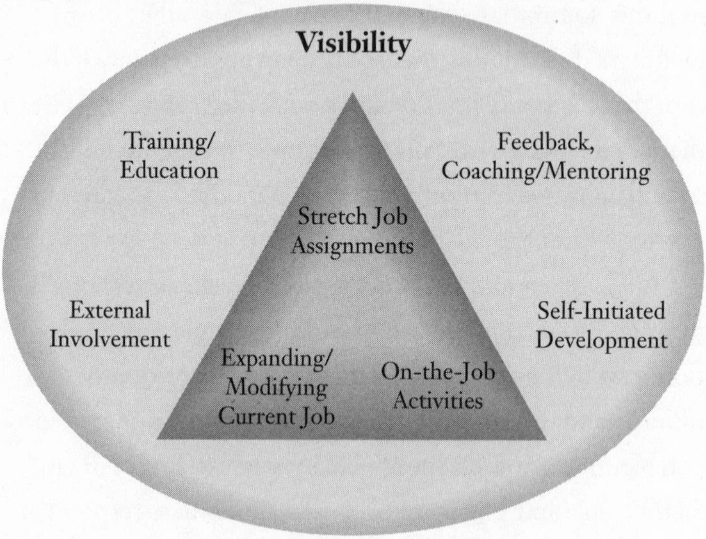

The triangle at the center of the model is intended to reinforce the fact that the core of your development springs from job experiences, especially stretch assignments—such as a move to a new business unit, from a line management role to a staff position (like Roberta Whiting experienced), or taking a leadership role in a much larger organization (like Paul Fairweather did)—or a significant expansion of your current role, as was the case with Bob Hendricks.

Although new assignments are what I call the red meat of career development, there will be times when you are relatively new in your position or the company's business priorities prevent you from moving to a new job. If that's the case, be mindful of the development opportunities you can pursue in your current role. Like the SVP who invited Fran Hopkins on an international market tour, managers in other parts of the company will frequently be extremely generous in orienting you to their areas—if you only ask. And as the case of Stu Clement illustrates, don't forget about opportunities to expand your skills and perspectives outside the company by taking on a leadership role in an industry or professional association or involvement with a civic or community group.

These kinds of development experiences won't come your way without effort on your part. So look for opportunities to increase your visibility within the company and build your network of relationships. Most often, it's the relationships you've formed that generate the spark that helps your career take off.

CHAPTER 10

Navigating Career Dilemmas

I f you're a talented, ambitious, and hard-working manager, you have every reason to assume that your career will be an up arrow. However, the higher you go in a company, the more competition there is for fewer slots and the more organizational realities come into play. In attempting to accomplish their career goals, aspiring executives like you often run into some difficult yet predictable career challenges. Having observed C-suite-level promotion decisions over the years, I would alert you to four especially knotty issues successful executives must navigate:

1. Keeping your ambition in balance with your commitment to the company

2. Dealing with a bad boss

3. Addressing a blockage situation

4. Deciding whether to stay with your company or seek greener pastures elsewhere

If you can successfully deal with dilemmas such as these, you'll be in a better position to accomplish your long-term career goals.

BALANCING AMBITION AND COMPANY COMMITMENT

In describing the unwritten rules in Chapter One, I highlighted several nonnegotiables and deselection factors. The nonnegotiable factors—the capabilities you must display to be considered as a candidate for the executive level—include your drive to lead and assume higher levels of responsibility. Central to that drive is a strong sense of ambition. That's the motor that makes you want to succeed and step up to the pressure that goes with the territory at the executive level. Realize that one of the deselection factors, putting self-interest above the good of the company, can create a potential conflict if your ambition to advance is not managed carefully. To be able to deal with this tension, you'll need to ensure that your motivation to succeed personally is never out of balance with the company's interests. You'll also have to be sensitive to your company's culture and its level of comfort with expressions of ambition.

In some companies, *ambition* is a dirty word—meaning that overt ambition is not well regarded. In other companies, people's drive to get ahead is not only expected, it's considered a positive trait. If you work for a company that is uncomfortable with direct expressions of ambition, you may have to couch your comments about promotion with some caveats—for example, stating your desire to advance to the executive level in terms like "at some time in the future," "under the right set of circumstances," or "assuming that I continue to perform and grow as a leader." In your career discussions, make sure you successfully communicate your career goals to the right people: those who can help you advance toward your career objectives or recommend you for the positions that will help you achieve them. Just make sure you convey your career goals in a manner consistent with your company's attitudes about ambition.

Regardless of your company's level of comfort with expressions of ambition, make a point of projecting a sense that your drive to succeed is fully in line with the interests of the company. In order to maintain the trust of the organization, you need to ensure that the actions you take are consistent with the company's goals so people are confident that you won't jeopardize the interests of the company for your own personal advancement. If you are able to do that on a day-to-day basis—and reinforce it in your career planning discussions—others will see you as an up-and-coming manager, the kind the company can rely on to lead it into the future.

DEALING WITH A BAD BOSS

It's a virtual certainty that at some point in your career you'll have a bad boss. Bad bosses come in a number of varieties, including the incompetent, insensitive, indecisive, and unfair. Some are meddling micromanagers. Some fold under pressure. Others may exhibit borderline or even blatantly unethical behavior. And some may be uninterested in your career progress or, worse, try to thwart it.

Interestingly, in their landmark study, *The Lessons of Experience: How Successful Executives Develop on the Job*, Morgan McCall, Michael Lombardo, and Ann Morrison found that having a bad boss was actually one of a future leader's most important development experiences.[1] Bad bosses helped the leaders studied learn approaches they didn't want to emulate as well as the fact that any manager will have shortcomings.

Dealing with a difficult manager is clearly a problem since your boss is a major factor in your ability to perform well in your job. And by virtue of his role, your boss should be a source of career feedback and support. Many managers with a bad boss adopt a "this too shall pass" attitude and try to wait it out until either they or the boss moves on to another assignment. Sometimes the relationship with the boss becomes so intense they are driven to risky extremes, like going to the boss's boss to demand that the manager be removed. Or they may jump ship and take a job with another company—frequently with negative consequences.

Realize that going to your boss's boss or a third party like HR rarely leads to a resolution in the short term. It's difficult for an individual subordinate to dislodge a boss, and your manager may have some special ability his boss values enough to tolerate what you see as poor management. Examples include a close relationship with an important customer or specific expertise the boss's boss lacks.

Since it's rare for a bad boss situation to be resolved overnight, I suggest you take some time and try to analyze the situation—especially if your relationship with the boss is causing strong emotions on your part. Use the techniques I discussed in Chapter Seven to build strong, positive working relationships with others. What are your boss's goals and interests? What does he value? How does he take in information (reading, verbally, in highly detailed reports)? How does he make decisions? By helping your boss achieve her goals and communicating in a way consistent with her preferred style, you are in a position to make a bad relationship at least acceptable for the time you report to her.

If your boss is being a micromanager, check to see if the area is new to him. Have you been able to establish your credibility with your boss as a reliable performer and team member? As we've observed, some bosses are chronic micromanagers who never give their people enough rope to do their jobs. Others loosen the reins once they've developed confidence in a direct report and feel they are getting the information they need to avoid being surprised.

Some direct reports try to stonewall a micromanager to show they are capable of running their own shop. I suggest you do the opposite. Especially if your boss is not well versed in your area, offer to educate her on the issues your department is dealing with. Ask what information she would like you to provide and what issues she's most interested in being informed about. On occasion—not always—your efforts to initiate communications will build the manager's confidence in you, and she'll begin to back off. Conversely, try to identify your boss's base of knowledge and expertise and convey a desire to learn from her. Sometimes when the boss feels valued, it helps you begin to build a relationship.

Importantly, don't allow yourself to get demoralized or drawn into commiserating with others about your boss. That will only cause you to take your eye off performing your job. Try to maintain your sense of professionalism and patience. Make sure your boss knows about your career goals and the conversations you've had with other executives about future career plans. Your boss may or may not agree with your career goals. However, informing your boss about past conversations makes it easier to continue your career discussions with other executives since it doesn't appear as if you're going around him. You have to be careful, but let those executives know of your interest in pursuing reassignment options—and sooner rather than later. Unless you know an executive well, avoid criticizing your boss directly, but let your tone communicate your strong desire to move on to the next developmental assignment. Sometimes an uptick in your sense of urgency to take on a new job will let others know it's time for them to intervene.

In some cases—and with the right steps on your part—a relationship with a bad boss will improve. Other times you or the boss will move on to other assignments. At the extreme you'll be forced to consider whether the experience is so negative you need to leave the company for another job. If you get to that point, I suggest you pay special attention to the "When the Grass Is Greener" section in this chapter.

ADDRESSING A BLOCKAGE SITUATION

You may have set your sights on a higher-level position on your path to advancement but find that position blocked by a long-tenured manager who doesn't look to be going anywhere soon. That manager may be a solid, if unspectacular, performer—someone with considerable institutional knowledge who is viewed as a rock of stability in the midst of organizational change—or someone preparing for retirement in a few years.

If you are confronted with this situation, my first suggestion is that you realize that many paths lead to career advancement. Although the position you've targeted may seem to be an ideal fit, this may be exactly the time in your career for a lateral move to another function or business unit within the company. If you do consider this kind of assignment, all of the conditions outlined for a lateral move in Chapter Nine still apply. However, if you can successfully engage the right group of executives, you may be able to gain an invaluable two to three years of experience and qualify yourself for higher-level positions you've never even thought of.

If you are viewed as a top performer your company wants to invest in, I've seen companies take highly creative steps to deal with a situation such as this—especially if it involves a manager who is interested in moving toward retirement. So if you spot an impending blockage situation, make a point to initiate a series of career discussions. Be sure to let others know the kinds of experiences you would find attractive and your level of flexibility in taking on a new assignment. For example, can you relocate? Is it feasible for you to consider an international assignment for a few years? By focusing on the kinds of experiences you'd like to have (a global assignment, a position close to the customer), and not just specific positions, you give the company more freedom to develop new options, perhaps creating a new position that doesn't currently exist. In the process, you can increase your skill level and make yourself an even stronger candidate for an executive-level position in the future.

WHEN THE GRASS IS GREENER: TO STAY OR LEAVE?

Most managers find bumps along their road in advancing to the C-suite level. Early in people's careers, promotions tend to come relatively quickly, but as you go higher up in the company, the pace of advancement usually slows. What's your situation? Perhaps you've been passed over for a promotion you thought should have come to you. Or you sense that your peers are moving ahead in their careers faster than you are. This raises an important question: Is it better to look outside your company to accomplish your career goals—or hope for the best where you are? It's not an easy question, and it demands a lot of thought on your part to get the answer right.

We've all seen managers who have left for greener pastures and had their careers take off. And you've probably witnessed your company hire people from the outside who achieve considerable success. However, moving to a new company in order to advance your career can be a slippery slope. Research on this topic is somewhat elusive, but most of the data I've seen suggest that the failure rate of those hired from the outside at the manager and executive levels is somewhere between 40 and 50 percent after twelve to eighteen months—and it probably exceeds 50 percent two years after hire.[2] That means you have, on average, a one out of two chance of things working out with a new company. Although looking outside your company to move forward in your career is not without risk, there are times when it makes sense to hit the escape hatch, especially if you take steps to shift the odds in your favor.

If you are concerned that your career progress is lagging, my first recommendation won't come as a surprise: contact those in your company who can provide you with the feedback that really counts. It's vital to know how you are perceived by those responsible for executive-level placements in your organization so you can plan accordingly. Too often I've seen managers get frustrated about not getting ahead in one company and jump ship to another—and then run afoul of the same issues that held them back in their prior organization. Examples include trouble collaborating with peers (which impedes your ability to work effectively across organization lines) or exhibiting deselection factors such as arrogance or insensitivity or taking a narrow, parochial perspective on the business.

As a rule of thumb, it's usually easier to tackle issues like these in your current company where you know the business and the other players. Don't underestimate the challenges of addressing them when you join a new organization. In assuming a job with a new company, there's a lot of pressure to learn the ropes in your new job, develop a new set of relationships, and show you can produce results. For most of us, stress tends to bring out our worst tendencies, so if there are aspects of your leadership or interpersonal style you need to work on, it's usually better to do it in your current job.

That said, there are times when you should explore the outside job market to identify other companies where you can increase your pace of career advancement. It's probably time to consider moving on if you confront these situations:

- You've been passed over multiple times and have not received feedback and guidance about the skills you need to display to move ahead in the future.

- You're locked in your current job by long-tenured people above you within the organization. If you have been unsuccessful in engineering a lateral move for development and have expressed your desire to see your career grow, the organization may implicitly be telling you that it's quite happy to see you continue in your current role.

- You've made a concerted effort to address the feedback you've received (for example, a need to rebuild the trust of your peers and coworkers), and you have not been successful in changing people's perceptions. It's a sad truth of organizational life that sometimes you have so much baggage from the past that it's virtually impossible to get people to see you in a new light, your best efforts notwithstanding.

If you are facing any of these situations, it's probably best to look at other companies, especially those with the kind of culture where you can succeed. In considering any new job, make sure you take the time to research the company thoroughly—its business, strategy, and culture—to determine if it's a fit for you in the long term. To do so, you'll need to go beyond what you pick up during the interview process. That tends to be an audition where both you and the company want to look your best.

If you've been successful in developing a strong network outside your company, this is the time to access it for information about a potential employer. Using your network, try to connect with former managers who worked for the company in the recent past. Assuming they will level with you, you'll get more candid insight into the company's culture and any political issues you may be walking into than you will from the company's recruiters. Dig deep to get a sense of how the company's culture matches your values. Is it a culture that promotes collaboration and collegiality or speed, urgency, and an individual's ability to put points on the board quickly? Is it highly innovative and fast moving, or does it value slow, methodical progress? Think carefully about what type of culture plays to your strengths.

If you've done this kind of due diligence and the job is right, you may have found a great fit for the long term. To maximize your chances of success, though, don't stop your developmental efforts when you walk through the door that first day on the new job. Find people in the new company who can provide you with early feedback over the first three or four months. If people are misinterpreting your intentions or see any behaviors on your part that go against the company's cultural grain, you'll want to know early on. That way you're in a position to take corrective action and make your partnership with the new company a good one.

Let me end on a cautionary note. A number of studies have looked at the factors that lie behind a manager's success or failure when joining a new company.[3] It's usually best to be moving *to* a new opportunity—as opposed to moving *away from* a poor job situation. So before you hit the escape button, I suggest you take the mirror test. Look candidly and objectively to identify what's holding you back in your company. If the reasons you're not getting ahead relate to the unwritten rules described in this book, more often than not, you'll find it easier to address them in your current organization. And by doing so, you'll avoid being part of the 50 percent of executives who don't succeed if and when you decide to join a new company.

THE REALITIES OF CAREER NAVIGATION

When senior executives talk about their careers, especially in public settings, they often mention how lucky they were to be in the right place at the right time. To some extent, they're being honest. Some of an executive's greatest career opportunities come her way unexpectedly and at favorable times. But don't be fooled entirely. Opportunities usually come your way as the result of hard work and preparation. Successful executives hone their skills in the course of their careers. And they learn—sometimes the hard way—to navigate the career obstacles they must face in order to make wise decisions along the way. You can't make the ideal job open up exactly when you want it. But by learning how to have productive career discussions with the right people and, in the process, teasing out feedback about any underlying concerns about your skills relative to the core selection factors, you'll be surprised by how often good things come your way.

CHAPTER 11

A Final Challenge to You—and Your Organization

I began this book with a desire to help you decode the unwritten rules—the poorly articulated factors companies use in making executive promotion decisions. Along the way, I've offered tips to ferret out feedback about where you stand in terms of those unwritten rules and suggestions on how to develop and display the core selection factors to build the confidence of senior-level decision makers in your company. Overall my goal has been to put you in a position to exercise greater control of your career.

Let me end with a final challenge to you, one based on the Golden Rule: Do unto others as you would have them do unto you. If you're a manager of others, start by remembering the times when you felt frustrated or were confused by the vague feedback you received about what you needed to do to progress in your career. If my suggestions have been helpful, take them to heart, and try to be the kind of boss you wish you'd had at important points in your career.

If you manage people today—and you will certainly do so as you move up in the organization—you'll work with talented employees who aspire to get ahead. As their manager, make sure they get the feedback that really counts—whether it's a skill required for success at the next level that they need to demonstrate or a pattern of behavior that could turn into a deselection factor if they don't address it. Help them find ways to get feedback from multiple sources, including those who will be involved in promotional decisions, and work with them to identify ways to display the required skills in their current job. If that's not possible, help them move to a new position where they will have the chance to develop and demonstrate the skills needed to advance in the company.

It's often said that each of us is responsible for our own career development. To a certain extent that's true. But as a manager, you play a pivotal role in helping others maximize their career potential. Over the years I've found that developing people typically takes a relatively small amount of a manager's time—if you focus on the right things. By helping others get the required feedback and making sure they are in a position to demonstrate critical skills, you'll have delivered on your most important development responsibilities.

I also believe that providing upwardly aspiring
managers with the feedback that really counts is the vital
first step in making corporate executive development
efforts more targeted and effective. This is critical because
most companies face a clear and present danger in
filling executive-level positions over the next few years.
Numerous studies indicate the challenges that companies
in the United States and Europe will face in replacing the
baby boomer executives who are in the process of retiring.[1]
The problem of executive succession is compounded by
a demographic reality: a gap in the number of managers
between thirty-five and forty-four years old in comparison
to the number of managers in the baby boom group who
are in the process of leaving the stage.[2]

Too often I see companies try to respond to this
impending leadership shortfall by offering broad-brush
leadership training programs in hopes of accelerating
the development of up-and-coming leaders. Curiously
I rarely hear the executives or high-potential managers
I work with say that such a leadership training program
was one of the most important development experiences
in their career. To help deal with this impending
shortfall of leadership talent, companies would be better
served by

- Cutting through the fog and specifying the most
  important skills required for advancement to the
  executive level, thus making them the written rules of
  executive success

- Providing people with candid and constructive feedback about where they stand in terms of those required skills

- Making sure they are in a position to develop and demonstrate those skills to the satisfaction of those who make executive promotion decisions

Today few companies do this well. However, I've seen it work, and the companies that learn how to do this enjoy a distinct advantage in building strong leadership within their ranks. For example, for years General Electric has conducted thorough assessments of candidates for corporate officer positions. Conducted by trained internal staff, these assessments collect a range of information about the potential executive from those who have worked closely with the person over the years. The results are summarized and shared with the individual so it is clear what the person's strengths are and what skills he or she needs to develop and display to advance to higher levels. GE makes a number of other investments in the development of its future executives, but the company's leadership assessment and development process pays big dividends in terms of GE's ability to develop strong leaders and fuel succession to executive positions.

Dell employs a comparable process for the managers it recruits into the company at middle levels and above. Approximately four months after a new manager joins

Dell, internal staff conduct in-depth interviews with the new manager's boss, peers, direct reports, and other coworkers. The new manager receives confidential feedback about the results, with particular emphasis on any "anti-Dell" behaviors that might get in the way of his or her success at the company. Over the past few years, Dell has been able to significantly reduce the attrition of new managers hired from the outside.

Approaches like the ones GE and Dell employ take courage—the courage to look a high-performing manager in the eye and tell her what she needs to do to advance in the organization. Executives in most companies are often uncomfortable with such conversations. They are concerned about demoralizing or losing a top performer. But in the absence of this feedback, the person's chances of progressing are sharply diminished, and that helps neither the individual nor the company.

Based on my experience and that of companies like GE and Dell, the willingness to provide this kind of feedback creates a win-win for companies committed to building leadership strength and for managers intent on furthering their careers. Companies gain by being able to take more focused and cost-effective development steps to accelerate the growth of their future executives. For upwardly aspiring managers, the benefits are a reduced sense of frustration and greater control in managing their careers. Armed with realistic feedback about where you stand in terms of your company's requirements for advancement, you'll have a better sense of where to devote your development efforts to get ahead.

I'll end with a story. Some years ago, I worked for a major division of a large corporation widely known for its ability to develop leadership talent. One day I was talking with Scott, the division's chief financial officer. In the course of our conversation, Scott looked me in the eye and said, "My biggest job is to develop someone who can do my job better than I can." Not as well as he could—better. I looked closely at him to see if he was serious, and he was. Dead serious. He went on to explain that the marketplace was becoming more intense and the division's long-range plan called for significant growth. So his successor would need to be better prepared than he was to lead the division's finance group into the future.

Scott was a great, results-oriented CFO, and he took his people development responsibilities seriously. He gave his direct reports candid feedback and didn't tolerate mediocre performance. He also challenged them and helped them move on to new jobs that advanced their careers. When he left the company, he had made good on his promise by having developed several highly talented finance leaders.

So keep Scott's words in mind as you move up to higher-level positions within the organization. At those levels, you take on greater responsibility for developing your company's next generation of leadership. If your bosses and others along the way have given you the feedback and support you've needed to succeed, return the favor. That attitude and the willingness to provide your staff with the feedback that really counts make a great senior leader.

CHAPTER ONE

1. This book is an expansion of my article, "Why You Didn't Get That Promotion: De-coding the Unwritten Rules of Corporate Advancement," *Harvard Business Review*, June 2009, pp. 101–105.

2. In the course of the book, I'll introduce case studies of managers I've worked with over the years. The individuals are real, but I've changed their names and certain details of the situation to ensure anonymity.

3. Examples of such research include Kevin Kelly, CEO of Heidrick & Struggles, who is quoted in B. Masters, "Rise of a Headhunter," *Financial Times*, Mar. 30, 2009, and B. Smart, *Topgrading: How Leading Companies Win by Hiring, Coaching, and Keeping the Best People* (Upper Saddle River, N.J.: Prentice Hall, 1999).

4. This impending shortfall in future executive talent is due to the fact that in both the United States and Europe, the demographic group of those aged thirty-five to forty-four, the one that organizations typically look to for new senior leaders, is currently some 18 percent less than the age group of the baby boomers who are in the process of retiring. This imbalance between supply and demand makes the rapid development of internal managerial talent a major priority in most large organizations. A. Barrett and J. Beeson, *Developing Business Leaders for 2010* (New York: Conference Board, 2002).

CHAPTER THREE

1. A word about terminology. Companies have a wide range of organization structures, but most combine a mix of business or operating units and functional units. Usually a business or operating unit is organized around a line of business and is

composed of a leader and a team representing a range of functions, such as sales, marketing, manufacturing, and customer service, dedicated to the business or operating unit. By contrast, a functional unit comprises staff with similar skills, such as finance, information technology, human resources, and legal. A functional unit may provide services on behalf of the entire company (for example, corporate finance) or support a variety of business units, but staff members typically report up to a head of the function, for example, chief financial officer, chief information officer, or general counsel.

CHAPTER FIVE

1. L. Bossidy and R. Charan, *Execution: The Discipline of Getting Things Done* (New York: Crown, 2002).

CHAPTER SIX

1. D. K. Murray, *Borrowing Brilliance: The Six Steps to Business Innovation by Building on the Ideas of Others* (New York: Penguin, 2009). C. Christensen, J. Dyer, and H. Gregersen, "The Innovator's DNA, " *Harvard Business Review*, Dec. 2009, pp. 60–67.

CHAPTER SEVEN

1. R. Cialdini, "Harnessing the Science of Persuasion," *Harvard Business Review*, Oct. 2001, pp. 72–79.
2. R. Fisher, W. Ury, and B. Patton, *Getting to Yes*, 2nd ed. (New York: Penguin, 1991).

CHAPTER NINE

1. A. Bryant, "Imagining a World of No Annual Reviews," *New York Times*, Oct. 18, 2009.

CHAPTER TEN

1. M. McCall, M. Lombardo, and A. Morrison, *The Lessons of Experience: How Successful Executives Develop on the Job* (New York: Free Press, 1988).

2. B. Masters, "Rise of a Headhunter," *Financial Times*, Mar. 30, 2009; B. Smart, *Topgrading: How Leading Companies Win by Hiring, Coaching, and Keeping the Best People* (Upper Saddle River, N.J.: Prentice Hall, 1999).

3. For example, B. Groysberg and R. Abrahams, "Managing Yourself: Five Ways to Bungle a Job Change," *Harvard Business Review*, Jan.-Feb. 2010, pp. 137–140.

CHAPTER ELEVEN

1. "US Human Capital Report, 2009/2010" (Saratoga Springs, N.Y.: PricewaterhouseCoopers Saratoga, 2010).

2. A. Barrett and J. Beeson, *Developing Business Leaders for 2010* (New York: Conference Board, 2002).

ACKNOWLEDGMENTS

A book such as this is the product of a career's worth of experience, observation, and the input of insightful people. In the early going, Kirsty Melville and Melinda Merino encouraged *The Unwritten Rules* project, and I'm grateful for their support. In preparation for writing this book, I spoke with twenty senior executives responsible for succession planning and filling executive-level positions in their organizations. Collectively they made a major contribution by testing and verifying my thinking. A number of people graciously devoted time to providing feedback on various chapters and thus helped strengthen the final result. I'm indebted to Tom Bowler, Lucien Alziari, Doranne Hudson, Eileen Whelley, Paul McKinnon, Shirley Gaufin, and Jim Shanley, as well as my Beeson Consulting colleagues: Kreig Smith, Lynn Litow Flayhart, and John Fulkerson. Genoveva Llosa of Jossey-Bass contributed at every step in the creation of this book. Her feedback and suggestions were invaluable in helping me put forward the concept of the unwritten rules—and what managers can do to develop and display them.

My greatest thanks go to the scores of CEOs, senior executives, and managers I've had the privilege to work with over the past thirty years. My conversations with CEOs and other senior executives provided insight into the factors that truly count when it comes to making C-suite promotion and placement decisions. Numerous executives shared with me the stories of their career progress: the skills they developed, how they developed them, and the pitfalls they experienced along the way. They are the true authors of this book.

ABOUT THE AUTHOR

John Beeson is principal of Beeson Consulting, a management consulting firm specializing in succession planning and top talent development, executive assessment and executive coaching, and organization design and change. Prior to founding Beeson Consulting, he was a partner and officer at Harbridge House, a Boston-based consulting firm specializing in management and organization development; director of management and organization development at Frito-Lay, a division of PepsiCo; and director of organization and human resource planning at Hallmark Cards. He was principal researcher and coauthor of a Conference Board research study, *Developing Business Leaders for 2010* and program director for its succession planning and top talent development seminar series, and he led its Organization Design and Renewal Conference. Beeson continues to speak at Conference Board conferences as well as periodic Webcasts. His articles on succession planning and talent development have appeared in the *Harvard Business Review*, *Across the Board*, and *Business Horizons*. He is a graduate of the Wharton Graduate School of Business at the University of Pennsylvania.

Page references followed by *fig* indicate an illustrated figure; followed by *t* indicate a table.

Career development strategies: Bob Hendricks's story on, 193, 197–198, 199, 205; building your external network, 183–184, 218; considering a lateral move, 184–186; demonstrating your learning ability, 190–192; engineering a development assignment, 187–190; identifying the right stretch assignment, 192–193; increasing your visibility within the company, 181–183; Jack Phillips's story on, 193, 195–197, 199; lessons to learn from stories on, 198–199; list of, 180; Paul Fairweather's story on, 193–194, 199, 205; Roberta Whiting's story on, 193, 194–195, 199; six core factors integrated into your, 179–180; taking responsibility for your own, 222–223

Career dilemmas: addressing a blockage situation, 213–215; balancing ambition and company commitment, 208–210; dealing with a bad boss, 210–213; overview of, 207–208; when the grass is greener: to stay or leave? 215–219

Career paths: developing strategies for, 179–205; lack of predictable, 1–2; realities of navigating, 219–220; taking responsibility for your own, 222–223

Challenging assignments, 82–83

Chambers, Tom, 26–31

Change. See Innovation and change capacity

Charan, Ram, 106

Christensen, Clayton, 121

Cialdini's reciprocity principle, 148

Citibank's No Guts, No Glory award, 127–128

Clement, Stu, 200, 202–204, 205

Coaching: to develop communication skills, 58; failing to stop micromanaging through, 91–94; strategy, 55

Collaborative capacity: building positive working relationships, 141–143; building strong management team to increase, 76–85; compensating for lesser strategic abilities by increasing, 60–63; as core selection factor, 15, 131–132. See also Competition; Lateral management

Colleagues: addressing and resolving conflict with, 149–152; building networks outside your organization, 183–184, 218; building positive working relationships with, 141–143; competition with, 132, 208–210; confidential interviews revealing opinions of your, 27–31, 92, 139–140; dealing with loss of trust by, 28–31; developing organizational and political understanding, 2–3, 143–146; developing your influence and impact on, 152; Golden Rule applied to interaction with your, 221–222; influencing and persuading your, 146–149. See also Organizations

Communication skills: active listening to feedback as, 34–36; to convey your strategic vision, 57–60; focusing on controllable factors for developing, 67; knowing how to ask and respond to feedback, 34–41; to motivate others to embrace new strategy, 62; quality of written e-mails and memos, 177; taking courses and coaching to improve your, 58. See also Public speaking skills

Index

F

Failure: being willing to experiment with, 124–126; creative people's attitude toward risking, 126–128
Fairweather, Paul, 193–194, 199, 205
Feedback: active listening to, 34–36; correcting erroneous information, 34; on failing to build a strong team, 75–76; getting to the core issues of, 35–36; used to improve executive presence, 162–166; inability to get helpful, 2; learning gene for ability to solicit, 191; manager role in your career conversation, 188–190, 212–213; Mike Peterson's story on receiving insufficient, 5–7, 8, 9; responding to, 36–41; that really counts, 21–41, 226–227; understanding the "code" of, 35. *See also* Confidential interviews; Job performance; 360-degree feedback surveys
Feedback barriers: desire not to demotivate, 23; inherent subjectivity of evaluation feedback, 22–23; lack of organizational consensus on skills/career potential, 23; tendency to assume that manager is incapable of further development, 24
Feedback that really counts: barriers to receiving, 22–24; developing future talent using, 226–227; how to ask for, 34–36; how to respond to, 36–41; importance of getting, 21–22; taking the initiative to get, 31; 360-degree survey barriers to providing, 25–26; 360-degree survey/confidential interviews providing, 26–31; who to ask,

31–34. *See also* Career conversations
Ferro, Tony, 111, 114–117, 124, 128
First lieutenant syndrome, 66–67
Fisher, Roger, 150
Follow-up mechanisms, 100–101

G

Gallagher, Craig, 71, 74–76, 83
General Electric (GE), 3, 224, 225
Getting promoted. *See* Executive advancement
Getting to Yes (Fisher, Ury, and Patton), 150
Global Technologies story, 2–8
Golden Rule, 221–222
Greener pastures, 215–219
Gregersen, Hal, 121
Gregory, Allen, 111, 117–130

H

Harvard Business Review, 121
Hastings, Gene, 161–166, 174
Henderson, Fred, 136–140, 148–149
Hendricks, Bob, 193, 197–198, 199, 205
Hopkins, Fran, 200–201, 205
HR (human resources) executives: bad boss dilemma and appealing to, 211; demonstrating strategic thinking as, 64; feedback role of, 33–34; Phil Whalen's story on failed development as, 48–51

I

Implementation management: as core selection factor, 14; receiving feedback to create strong team, 75–76
Increasing visibility, 181–183
Industry perspective: abstract thinking to improve your, 54; broadening your, 53–54; learning about trends to broaden your, 55–56;

241